ADVENTURES

IN

THE LIGHT

From the diary of

Nathalie de Wet

NATHALIE DE WET

Copyright © 2022 Nathalie de Wet

FIRST EDITION - REVISED

All rights reserved.

No part of this publication may be reproduced, stored, distributed, or transmitted by any form or by any means, including photocopying, recording, or other electronic or mechanical methods, without prior written permission of the Publisher or author, except in the case of brief quotations in critical reviews and certain other non-commercial uses permitted by copyright law.

Disclaimer: It was not the author's intention to defame anyone. Full names of people have been left out wherever possible. Where real names have been used it is to honour the individuals mentioned, not to defame anyone or their character. No defaming insults are intended towards any religious group, Political group, Race or Culture, the South African Police, or the world of Mental Health. The opinions expressed are expressed in a time of "freedom of speech" before "political correctness."

Publisher   Nathalie de Wet QLD 4506, Australia ABN 93509640962

Edited   by Grammarly, Z Read and Elliot Sunflower

ISBN   978-0-6487484-4-1 Paperback

ISBN   978-0-6487484-5-8 Digital version

Cover design: "Crossing Over" by Nathalie de Wet – prints are available for sale through the author. See Contact the Author page.

ADVENTURES IN THE LIGHT

Dedicated to His Majesty,

I'm humbled by Your love and forgiveness.

Thank you for loving me and

for helping me to do this.

CONTENTS

- BOOK REVIEWS 1
- PREFACE 3

PART 1: THE FIRST BEING IN THE LIGHT 9
- 1. SEEING JESUS 10

PART 2: JESUS 24
- 2. WOULD THE REAL JESUS PLEASE STAND UP? 25
- 3. THE GOOD SHEPHERD 31
- 4. THE HARMONY OF THE GOSPELS 40
- 5. IMAGINARY FRIEND 42

PART 3: MY BACKGROUND 48
- 6. INTO THE FOREST 49
- 7. MY CHURCH HISTORY 52
- 8. WHAT IS BEING 'BORN AGAIN'? 54
- 9. WATER BAPTISM 55
- 10. BAPTISM IN THE HOLY SPIRIT 65
- 11. CATCH THE FIRE 73
- 12. THE GOLD DUST STORIES 77
- 13. PERSPECTIVE 82

PART 4: ANGELIC BEINGS IN THE LIGHT 87
- 14. ANGELS ON THE CEILING 88
- 15. GOING TO HAWAII 100
- 16. A LEAP OF FAITH 123
- 17. THE CENTRE OF THE WORLD 126

- 18. WOULD THE REAL GOD PLEASE STAND UP 130
- 19. RELIGION IS MESSY 136
- 20. THE DARK SIDE 140

PART 5: THE LIGHT 148
- 21. THE NEAR-DEATH EXPERIENCE 149
- 22. INSIDE THE LIGHT 170
- 23. THE UNIVERSAL LOVE 175
- 24. YOU ARE A MYSTIC! 176
- 25. THE ANGEL IN MY HOUSE 180
- 26. OUR WEDDING AND HIS FUNERAL 182

PART 6: GIFTS FROM HEAVEN 187
- 27. HEARTS FROM HEAVEN. 188
- 28. HEALING IS FOR TODAY 199
- 29. THE KEYS 201

PART 7: CONCLUSION 210
- 30. APPOINTED TIME TO DIE 210
- 31. THE GREATEST GIFT HE GAVE ME 213
- 32. COMFORT IN DEATH 223
- 33. THE MEANING OF LIFE 224

REFERENCES USED/STUDY GUIDE 225

ABOUT THE AUTHOR 235

ADVENTURES IN THE LIGHT

Based on a true story

from the autobiography **DISCOVERING AN ARTIST**

an inspirational true story from Nathalie's Journals

By NATHALIE DE WET

BOOK REVIEWS FOR DISCOVERING AN ARTIST

"I found this book to be a "Book of Miracles" and incredible faith, waiting for instructions and provision of every need, however small or unimportant it may seem"– Zandra Read, First editor of Discovering an Artist 2010

"A very moving and sometimes raw account of a story seen through the eyes of an artist. While sometimes sad, the story is laced with hope and miracles. You will be encouraged by the tenacity and courage of the Artist who shares her story with you." - review on Discovering an Artist, Trish Jenkins, International Author/ Change & Resilience Speaker

BOOK REVIEWS FOR ADVENTURES IN THE LIGHT

To be added in future editions. Please send your reviews to nathaliesstudio@gmail.com

To help you understand my writing style:

Handwriting (font may appear as italics) has been used to express a hand-written journal entry, which I made in journals; and italics have been used the JeffMara Podcast extracts and Bible scripture references.

Italics. I understand that I have not used them entirely correctly for grammatical purposes. I have tried to use them to express *thoughts and conversations with the reader.* Also, thoughts, *in retrospect.*

CAPITAL LETTERS have been used to express something I heard God say with my ears audibly, like a voice behind me speaking to me, or with a STRONG IMPRESSION. I have also used them to express lighter impressions, but feeling it was God speaking to me. For example, driving passed a billboard sign and seeing the words, "ART WITH ALTITUDE." The words were written on a billboard-sign, but they 'quickened inside of me,' as if jumping out and speaking to me. I believe this to be a 'prompting of the Holy Spirit' and another form of God speaking to me.

I've also used capitals as DIVISION headings and HEADINGS, and names of places as I travelled. Other **sub-headings** are in sentence case.

The Australian English Language setting has been used. This affects American spelt words like, Honor – Honour, neighbor – neighbour

PREFACE

My name is Nathalie (Natalie). I'm a shy introvert and I don't want to write this book. I would rather be painting right now, but I'm being pulled by the spiritual forces that drive me to do crazy little things, so here I am, writing this book for you. Telling you my story (again) but **from a different perspective,** with some practical steps that I took, that you can take too, to see extraordinary, unusual, and supernatural provision manifesting in your life. *What?* I know, how did I get our family car for $9? Extraordinary stories. Unusual and supernatural provision is the way I live and how I am training my children and others. It's called *living in the miraculous* and *walking by faith*. If you want a taste of it, you may enjoy my books.

In my autobiography, *Discovering an Artist*, I wrote my life story chronologically from birth until 1999. In 1999 I had a NDE (near-death experience, out of body spiritual experience), which opened a whole new chapter or a new book for me. It is a good place to end the story.

Walking the reader through my process of "self-discovery," seeing that I was not a schoolteacher, nor a missionary but in fact born an Artist. Hungry to paint. I briefly touched on the religious/spiritual side. Delving into the possibility of becoming a full-time Christian missionary meant that I had to deal with the topic of "religion." There were some supernatural things and visions, that occurred during my travels, but I rushed through them quickly. I thought that it was not going to be something that I would ever speak to people about in detail; they would think I was crazy! (Christians were not very tolerant of such things, but it remained in the back of my mind. I kept doing crazy things and I kept learning.)

About ten years ago I began speaking more about these unusual things. After I published the autobiography, some people became curious and would ask me to explain or elaborate on the things that I'd rushed over.

I introduced the reader to my idealistic paradise: our family home, the setting of the book. When I was entering into my schooling years, my parents bought their first home. I stayed on that same property from 1979 until

1999, off and on, moving back in 1999 until I got married. It was a paradise, **through the eyes of a child**. It had many hideaway places to play a game like hide-and-seek. Also, home to many interesting animals like scorpions, snakes, owls, and bats, as well as our family pets.

Now I will introduce you to it from another perspective. **Through the eyes of an adult**, it was an abandoned piece of ground. People had vandalised the buildings. The old house was broken. No windows. No electricity. No carpets. No doors. No cupboards. Long grass covered the acre. My parents were able to purchase it and had to work multiple jobs to afford the renovations and pay off the mortgage, which they did in about 7 years.

It took twenty years to fix it. My dad got some paint called "biscuit" but on a large scale, the whole house looked like it was painted an ugly pumpkin brown-orange.

Initially we stayed there with no electricity. Boiling kettles of water to have what my mother called a 'bird bath.' Our father loved nature and camping, well kitted out and equipped for camping in his skillset. We were cold sometimes, especially in the freezing Johannesburg winters, but survival and bathing by candlelight were all part of the adventure. We lived in a good suburb and that was worth the struggle, in my eyes. As long as nobody saw where I lived and the condition of the house. I never invited a single person over for at least the first seven years. I was too embarrassed about our 'pumpkin house'. Do you know the story of Cinderella? She rushes home and the carriage turns back into a pumpkin before she can make it home. She had looked like a princess, but the sombre truth was that without the mystical magic, she was in a pumpkin.

After I finished school, I left home immediately and began considering the possibility of becoming a full-time Christian missionary. I worked, studied part-time, and travelled.

I went around Africa learning to love different people, doing "mercy missions" (feeding the poor). Travelling into Zambia to learn about mass Evangelism, (preaching to people, feeding people spiritually). Across to North America and Hawaii, then on to Europe and the Middle

East. Backpacking on several overseas trips, over several years. I returned to my parents' home after I was attacked, to heal from the injuries that I'd received during the attack. I remained there until I got married.

In this book, I explain what I was not able to explain in the first book. I delve deeper into explaining the beings in the light and the Light itself. I tell you, the reader, the things I have now told thousands of people. I say thousands with confidence because, on 7th of 7th 2022, I was interviewed by Jefferey Reynolds on his Paranormal 'JeffMara' Podcast #522; within a week it had been viewed by twenty thousand people.

Many who have experienced near-death experiences and spiritual encounters, have similar stories. Yet each story is unique. With modern medicine bringing more people back from near-death, there is an increase in these stories, and people like me, are now more comfortable to speak out, than we were twenty years ago.

Enjoy my spiritual adventures, as much as I have enjoyed living it.

Nathalie

My husband-to-be grew up in another Province of South Africa. Growing up in a coastal province, near the ocean, not in the middle of the country, in the highveld where I lived. By car, at least six hours drive from each other.

PART 1: THE FIRST BEING IN THE LIGHT

Title: Come as you are   Painting by Nathalie de Wet

Can I start by just telling you how beautiful Jesus is? With no Christianity, no religion, no background knowledge. He just came to me in my bedroom, and that is how I found Him, because He found me first.

1. SEEING JESUS

I had a stable childhood. One preschool, one Primary school, and one High School. One home throughout all my schooling. Nothing traumatic happened to me that required me to create an actual "imaginary friend" of tutelary[1] function to ease some childhood anxieties. *'as a guardian angel to watch over and protect.'*
[1]

I was cute. Alive to dreaming. I used to have dreams that seemed very real. It would feel like my 'body' was leaving through the window and going to another place.

This could have been just another dream, but this one was different. I was awake.

Journal entry. Recalling a 'vision' from about 1979:

It was night. I'm guessing it was late in 1979, based on what I have gathered. I'm guessing it was 3am, because most spiritual encounters seem to happen for me at exactly 3am. I went to the toilet. I came back into my bedroom.

I was suddenly caught up into an "open vision." *(I will attempt to explain exactly what that is later.)*

My soul-spirit was in this place, it was like a forest, but it was like a maze, not the forest I would normally dream about, or perhaps it was, but a section of it that I had not yet ventured into.

It was a dark forest. It had worn pathways or passages between the trees. I was running through the maze pathways, as if I was searching for a way out. Trying to find the exits. The maze had no exits. At every exit was an image which reminded me of a 'danger sign' (skull with crossbones). No entry.

I wasn't being chased. I felt trapped. Unable to get out – but not scared or terrified, like a nightmare. Just unable to find The Way out.

This process probably lasted a few minutes.

Overwhelmed by the situation. I stopped and dropped onto my knees. *Both physically in the natural and in this open vision.*

It felt like I was giving up.

I heard a voice speaking to me.

We adults analyse everything. *'Was the voice external?' 'Did I hear it with my ears or inside me?'* I cannot recall. Maybe it was an inner voice. Maybe an external one. What I do recall is that it felt like it was coming from behind me. It wasn't my own thoughts. I was too focused on the search.

The voice behind me said:

"THE ONLY WAY OUT, IS UP"

With that I looked up.

I was now fully in my bedroom. I was not in the maze.

From that moment I was back in my bedroom. Back in my body. Back in the natural realm. I was no longer in the vision of the forest. This is where I saw "The Thing" that my Dad would later come to call my "imaginary friend."

In front of me stood a man.

He was like a spiritual type of vision. Not a hologram. It was like seeing a person standing in your bedroom, solid like a person, not see-through. But your mind knows, or thinks it knows, that there is not really someone standing in your bedroom. Your mind is fighting to comprehend it.

He was surrounded by pure white light. The white light He was surrounded by was a brilliant white but didn't hurt your eyes. It was not like being in a dark room and turning on an artificial light which shocks your eyes, and you squint. It was gentle on the eyes, but so incredibly white. Whiter than the whitest white you know. I have tried to paint it, but white paint is not white enough to express the whiteness of the white!

He was not on the floor. He was standing a bit elevated off the floor, but he went through the ceiling. It was like matter, the world that we see, did not matter. Like he transcended matter. I saw Him in the natural realm, but it was like He could transcend this realm. Be in two realms at once. The ceiling was not an obstruction. He just went right through it.

When you see someone standing off the ground, you think your eyes are playing tricks on you. Your mind is trying to figure it out. I think He was just giving me time to patiently take it all in. But it was mere seconds before I spoke out in a gasp.

I thought at first that this "vision" was a still picture. When people talk about seeing "a vision" I imagine that they are speaking about "still pictures." I suddenly knew that this was a living moving being, not a still picture. He smiled at me.

My Spirit knew who this being was, my Soul did not know, but my Spirit did. By "my Soul", I mean, I, Nathalie, my personality, I had no idea who He was, but my Spirit, my "Light" body, knew. Out of my mouth came an exclamation of adoration, "JESUS!" and my whole body bowed down, as if meeting a King or bowing to the Queen. My arms went up into the sky as if on autopilot! My ears heard my mouth, and it was like, "Oh, is that who it is?" I also got quite a fright because I had said it so loudly that I even made myself jump! My sister was in the bedroom as we shared a bedroom. I remember quickly looking across toward my sister to see if I had woken her and still having my arms flung up towards the sky.

I looked back at Him. He was just standing there. He held His hands open to me. He was wearing some type of white robe. *(Since then, I've travelled to the middle east. It reminds me now, of the middle eastern clothing.)*

He smiled at me. It was a gentle smile.

He had brown hair and a brown beard and moustache. I didn't like moustaches but his didn't seem to bother me. I was drawn by his loving eyes. I was wrapped up in the love. His eyes radiated love. His eyes, big brown eyes. *(I did not see blue or green eyes as some other accounts have observed).*

I saw the scars on the base of his palms. *(I did not see blood in his hands).* I had no idea who He was, nor anything about His crucifixion at that stage. All I knew was that my Spirit knew who He was, and His name was obviously, "JESUS"…, whoever that was.

After this I went to sleep.

Being that close to Jesus, you will understand that there is NO GREATER LOVE, NO GREATER JOY, NO GREATER PEACE, NO GREATER ANYTHING. He is amazing.

I woke up the next morning and I asked my father, "Who is Jesus?" and we got talking about the vision. Coming from a non-religious family, I was not told who Jesus was from a Christian perspective.

I did not envisage that sharing my little vision with others would help anyone else.

My uncle had once remarked that 'religion is a personal and private' matter. I kept quiet concluding that everyone had their own journey, and that it was private.

The memory of my vision of Jesus never left the screen of my imagination over time. When we try recalling a dream, it fades. Spiritual experiences and spiritual dreams don't seem to have an expiry date. They come back to me when I think about them. Not with as much vividness as when they happened, but still with more clarity than trying to recall a dream. I feared that if I shared this experience, it would fade away.

Because you have seen me you have believed. Blessed are those who have not seen me and have believed.

John 20:29

A warning from Jesus

I do not believe that every "Christ-like appearance" is Jesus or even "of God," for that matter. I also do not believe that we will "see Jesus in the flesh," as some claim, until He *descends* back to earth. He is up there, where He went when He left here. We are warned quite firmly in the Bible, about this coming deception. It was coming and I think still is to come. I'll put the warning in my own words, and you can go and read the whole chapter, which can be found in Matthew chapter 24.

Jesus said we need to be careful of the deception that was coming. That many would come and talk about him or "Christs" and some would even come claiming to be him, "The Christ or Messiah or another Jesus." Some people would believe these false deceptions.

He said false prophets and false teachers were coming. They would deceive many. Even have false signs and wonders. Vultures gather where there is something rotten.

(In Acts, Corinthians, and Galatians we are told of the Holy Spirit's true signs and wonders, and fruit; in Jesus' life we are told the true signs and wonders that followed His earthly ministry. Humility is a BIG KEY to the true signs).

Some would say Jesus is here or there – but don't go

running around trying to find where He was. Because when He did come back, which He would, every single person would see His return and every knee would bow, (regardless of if they believed in Him) because even the demons know He is the King of Kings and the Lord of Lords.

Open visions

When Steven was being stoned[2] he saw Jesus or Jesus was revealed to him, as the "heavens opened." When you see 'a vision' or see into this other realm you may experience an "open vision."

Another example to explain what it is like for the experiencer: if you are in a planetarium and they are shining the dark sky onto the ceiling, and you look up. You are on the inside, but it feels like you are on the outside, like you are looking at the stars.

I read a description of an "open vision" in a book. It was the first time that I had heard someone describe *"How I received the vision"* and it was similar to my own experience. I have since read definitions elsewhere, but in California while planning to write my autobiography, I wrote to the author asking for his permission to use his explanation in my book, so here it is quoted with written permission.[3]

Page 9: There are many levels of prophetic revelation. The beginning levels include prophetic "impressions" Page 10: "Open visions occur on a higher level than impressions; they tend to give us more clarity than we may have even when we feel the conscious presence of the Lord, or the anointing. Open visions are external and are viewed with the clarity of a movie screen. Because they cannot be controlled by us, I believe that there is far less possibility of mixture in revelations that come that way.

Another higher-level prophetic experience is a trance, such as Peter when he was first instructed to go to the house of Cornelius and preach the gospel to the Gentiles for the first time and such as Paul had when he prayed in the temple in Acts 22. Trances were a common experience of Biblical prophets. Trances are like dreaming when you are awake. Instead of just seeing a "screen" like in an open vision, you feel like you are in the movie, that you are there in a strange way. Trances can range from those that are rather mild, so that you are still conscious of your physical surroundings, and even still interact with them, to those where you feel like you are literally in the place of your vision. This seems to be what Ezekiel experienced frequently, and what John probably experienced when he had the visions recorded in the book of Revelation."

It wasn't a dream. I was awake. I'd just come back from the toilet. I was interacting with this place. Based on the description, I would say it was some type of "open vision," "higher level than impression" or a "trance."

The best way for me to explain this experience, is to say my soul-spirit was out of my physical body, hovering above it, a sensation of 'levitation' above the bed and then it went back inside my body.

Since this experience, I have had a different OBE (Out of Body experience)[4] associated with nearly dying. Having experienced a fuller OBE, where my soul-spirit was floating around perceiving what was going on in various rooms, I would say that this was not an "OBE" even though my soul-spirit was obviously hovering above and outside of my body.

I was not on any medication. I've heard from some, that

they don't believe we have an 'out of body' experience; but merely that the brain *alters our perception of our reality.* It's believable for me, for someone to think this, as when I've read or heard some near-death experience accounts, sometimes the person took a drug overdose, or they were on medication in the hospital. Their "spiritual experience" sounds like a "trip" or an *altered state of reality*.

Once when I was on morphine after surgery, I experienced an altered mind perception on things. In that experience, I did not feel like my spirit was sitting *outside* of my physical body. I still felt connected, inside, my body. My mind was perceiving things that were not there. My mind imagined my husband was standing outside the room talking on the other side of the wall. I would call that an "altered mind perception."

For me, when I speak of "out of body," my spirit was a white light moving away from my physical body, *separate* from it. It felt separate and almost disconnected, being outside of my physical body. Perhaps those who say we are connected by a silver thread are correct, but I never saw a silver thread.

How you choose to interpret this experience, which I will call "a vision," is up to you. For me asking "how" and "what" and "why" this happened, was not as important as the "WHO" I saw.

I've also been told that what I experienced was a Theophany - "a visible manifestation to humankind of God or a god."[5] This makes sense to me, to call it a Theophany.

Spirit-body/light-body

I grew up in Africa. Africans are spiritual. African religions share a common belief in a Supreme Being, and a belief in the realm of the spirits. Usually, these 'spirits of the ancestors' reveal themselves through dreams. The old South Africa had a dominant conservative Christian culture. To the conservative Christians, if anything revealed itself in any form, it was generally considered to be *a demonic spirit* appearing to deceive you.

Amongst the Zulu (AmaZulu) Healers, the *inyanga* (medicine-men) primarily uses herbs, while the *isangoma* (Witchdoctor) is primarily concerned with the spirit. Sickness is seen as a whole person sickness: body and spirit as the Zulu do not separate the physical body and the spirit. To the Christians, these men were both considered evil. The one was seen as 'bad' with their herbs and potions, and the other was seen as 'bad' for being spiritually evil, working with sorcery and magic. Neither were considered 'good' only Christians were considered 'good.'

I see us humans as being made up of three parts: THE BODY, THE SOUL, and THE SPIRIT.

The material BODY is the physical. A 'clay' vessel that deteriorates, gets old and dries up, then dies or sleeps in the cold ground.

The SOUL is our individual personality, it is eternal. It departs from the Body when we die. It lifts out of our body in a traumatic near-death experience. *I am speaking from experience on that.* The Soul can become awakened. Elevate its thoughts. Receive divine inspiration. The Soul holds the mind, will and emotions. If the Soul is sick the body gets sick. The Bible refers to this part of us as "Our flesh" with its "fleshly desires" - it is the desires of the mind and emotions not the desires of the skin, bones, and meat.

Our SPIRIT is the part of us that connects to 'the Greater Light' which Jewish mystics call, *"Ein Sof"* - "The Infinite" I think that is a fitting description. Perhaps you could call it "The Primary Light" or "The Source." Our Spirit is eternal. It is free. It has understanding. The Spirit carries a special energy, a life force. Life itself is in it. It is also the Light or our "Light-body." Connected to the Primary Light.

PART 2: JESUS

Title: The Crucifixion of Jesus   Oil painting by Nathalie de Wet 2019

2. WOULD THE REAL JESUS PLEASE STAND UP?

This 'vision' of Jesus in Part 1 happened before I went to school. Before I knew anything about Jesus, the Christ, the Crucifixion, and the Jews.

Something that I struggled with reconciling in my mind, was that the "Jesus" that I saw, had dark hair, a beard and a moustache and brown eyes. The Jesus I had seen, was strong, and He had big, strong hands. The "Jesus" that I was being presented with in school, in the artwork and pictures, was this blonde-haired skinny guy… "The Christ." He looked frail and had blue eyes.

I concluded, *"I don't know who that is,"* because he was not **my Jesus** that I had seen, or that my Spirit knew. I called him, the 'Christian Jesus' and "The Christ." 'The Christ' seemed like 'another Jesus'. Maybe this is exactly what Jesus was referring to in Matthew 24? That people would misrepresent Him in future generations and present 'another Jesus'. Maybe it is only part of the deception and there is more to come.

I knew that "The Christ" was a man (human); like Buddha

was a man. Joseph Smith was a man. Mohammad was a man. I did not know that Jesus was *a Jew*. I had learned from observations of artwork, that He was a pale white man, with blonde hair and blue eyes.

Christians and Jews

Around me, it seemed that everybody said that they were 'Christians' if they weren't Jews. Jews were held in low regard it seemed, by the Christians. We were all 'Christians' because the 'Jews' apparently lived together near the synagogue. So, by deductive reasoning, based on where I lived, I must have been a "Christian."

My Dad used a few Jewish phrases. He was more than once referred to as, "Jew-boy" by his 'friends' or clients. I understood it was because of his prominent nose feature. I did not think it had anything to do with being "Jewish."

People did not get 'born again' or 'become a Christian' – by 'believing in Jesus' or making a commitment to serve Him. Everybody was a "Christian." When I started hearing about being "born again" or being a "born again Christian" it seemed like a new fad. I did not know it was a spiritual rebirth that they had found in the Bible.

Like the misleading teachings about 'Jews' being evil (the murderers of Jesus), 'The Lord's Prayer'[6] wasn't taught to me correctly either. The line which says, "lead us not into temptation" I was taught God tempts us. He was quite a nasty, old man. God got blamed for everything! Besides it says, *"When tempted no one should say, 'God is tempting me.' For God cannot be tempted by evil, nor does He himself tempt anyone; but each one is tempted when, by his own evil desire, he is dragged away and enticed."* [7]

Who was this "Christian Jesus"? The Christ.

I had no idea. I'd heard of him, but I had never met <u>the man</u>. I knew he was a male. I didn't know what his voice sounded like. I knew about him. There was a birth which people celebrated at Christmas. We did not really celebrate Christmas. We did not have a nativity set, nor do anything 'traditional' or what 'church Christians' did. Some shops had nativity scenes, but generally in most nativity scenes, he was stripped of all his 'Jewish-ness' and displayed a blonde "Christ" baby-Jesus.

Journal entry many years later while I was living in California.

Journal USA California 1998:

I'm sitting in California as I write this. I was challenged by some Jewish people I've met here to reconsider my thoughts about Jewish people. They told me I was "anti-Semitic." I didn't even know what that meant I had to go look it up! "Anti-Jew or Arab." They challenged me to read this book called "The Last Sunrise" by Harold Gordon a Holocaust survivor, and to watch a movie called, "Schindler's List" (1993). So maybe they were right. Maybe I have been "Indoctrinated" with some "anti-Jew" ways of thinking.

I can see now that I needed to go to the USA to meet the Jewish family that I met, because I had to learn to love Jewish people. They were so kind to me. Patient with me. God would later take me to Israel and Israel is full of Jewish people!

Later Journal entry, 2010:

I've learnt that people try to strip Jesus of his Jewishness. He is Jewish! A descendant of King David, "the Son of David." I think therefore they painted Him with blue eyes and why the Preface of the Bible tells us they removed words like "Messiah" and "Adonai," "Elohim" YHVH/YHWH (Tetragrammaton) etc. replaced* with LORD and Christ."

*Read the preface of most Bibles for details on this.

From my diary about Jesus' eyes in my Art.

Journal 2005 New Zealand:

I entered a National Art competition in New Zealand. I asked the Lord if I could win it because I desperately wanted to win the money so that I could open a bank account in New Zealand. He said "I ALREADY HAVE A WINNER" – so I made my peace with the 'fact' that it wasn't me and that whoever really needed to win it would win it. Instead of painting for the money I shifted my focus and painted out of love for Him. I painted a lion/man and called it "Matthew 13:13" It was my representation of Jesus, the Lion of Judah.

A lady saw it and suggested that if it was representing Jesus, I should paint Him with blue eyes to represent that He was a Saint. Immediately I felt uncomfortable about that. I didn't know why and so I prayed. When I asked Him what to do, He answered clearly, "WHAT COLOUR DO YOU SAY MY EYES ARE?" "Brown" I answered without hesitation, stating the obvious, and sensed He was smiling.

I knew His eyes were brown because I had seen Him very clearly when I was younger. I never doubted seeing Him.

 nathaliesstudio

Title: Matthew 13:13   Painting by Nathalie de Wet 2005

Subject: Lion/Man – Brief: Interpreting a parable.

1st place winner, in National competition in New Zealand 2005. Original painting was sold to a collector.

Matthew 13:13 "I speak to them in parables because while

seeing they do not see, while hearing they do not hear, nor do they understand"

In case you're curious and haven't already caught onto this: I was the 1st place winner of the National competition that He had chosen! I discovered it at the Art exhibition in the city when my sister pointed it out, to my great surprise! The letter to inform me had been delayed by the sender attending a funeral. The prize money was the exact amount that I required to open the bank account in New Zealand.

3. THE GOOD SHEPHERD

I don't want to point you to Christianity. I want to point you to Jesus.

Jesus was Jewish.

I don't want to point you to Judaism because it is a religion focused mainly on the Talmud and they don't believe Jesus is the Messiah.

Jesus is not just a man; therefore, I don't want to point you to Islam and the Qur'an.

I very clearly do not want to belong to any of these major Religions of the World. Therefore, each one tells me, that I'm condemned to "Hell" or whatever the place is, that they call it. The temporary or permanent place *they feel they aren't going to.*

The truth is that when we die, we go into the unknown!

I don't know where they are going! I am going to be with Jesus! I love Him and I KNOW that He loves me. I know it! I do not doubt it. He was there the last time that I almost died, and He will be there again! He loves me so much.

For God so loved the world that He gave His Only begotten Son, Jesus, that whoever believes in Him shall not perish but have eternal life. [8]

Guess what? He didn't die on the cross for *Nathalie*. He died on the cross for HUMANITY. The cross was not for nothing.

You can get to know Him. Just ASK HIM. It's your choice,

your free will to talk to Him.

> *"Sing unto God praises to His name extol Him that rides upon the Heaven by His name YAH and rejoice before Him."* [9]

Jesus is YAH. He is God.

God said to Moses to tell the people that He was "I AM WHO I AM." [10]

Christians call God, Father. Jesus said, "No one comes to the Father except through me" Jesus also said, *"I and the Father are one." "I am in the Father and the Father is in me." "If you really knew me you would know."* [11]

Jesus, (Yeshua, Yahushua or YAHShua[12]) in my understanding IS the Father in the form of man. God incarnate. I was told by someone that the Apostle Paul created this idea, but I clearly see this in John's gospel quoted above, not from the teachings of Paul.

The angels are always saying, 'Holy Holy Holy'[13] before the throne, but 'Heaven was silent for half an hour.'[14] It would make sense that they were silent because God was not there. In my understanding, He left and came down. The

Holy Spirit overshadowed Mary and she became pregnant with God in the form of a man. That was the half an hour when God left heaven or maybe the whole life of Jesus 33 years was only half an hour in Heaven! Time is very different in the spiritual realm. We are told 'a day is like a thousand years and a thousand years is like a day'. I know for myself the time did not feel like they were in the same time zone between the two realms.

I can tell you that Jesus is the most widely written about person in history; described as the most influential person who ever lived. **He cannot be contained!**

All religions point to Him in some way or another; through forbidding you to read Isaiah 53, forbidding personal relationship or by teaching *about* Him and not teaching you to get to *know* Him.

I'm not claiming to be God's messenger delivering a new religion to you. There are many people across the world who believe what I believe: Jesus is God.

The Messianic believers I've met so far (aka "Believers") believe Jesus, Yeshua, the Messiah, the anointed one, is God sent to earth. They showed me how it was God in *the form of a man* on earth through the meaning of Hebrew words and culture.

In Christianity we sing that He will be called Wonderful, Counsellor, the Everlasting Father, yet some people get annoyed if I call Him "The Everlasting Father" stating that he was just the Son who had a Father. That is putting it into human boxes to try and comprehend it.

God is bigger than our mind. He is vaster than our comprehension. He came down HIMSELF because there is no way that he would have sacrificed his own "child" He is not a murderous father! In the same way that He did not expect Abraham to go through with sacrificing Isaac. He is loving. He is kind. God made Himself the offering, but the soldiers couldn't even take him. He had to hand Himself over to them and hand Himself over to death. If you don't believe me, go read the arrest account. They were "slain in the spirit" (fell flat on their faces) as soon as He said I AM.

When He rose, there was a real life "zombie apocalypse" that we don't see mentioned in the "Jesus" movies. Dead people came out of their graves. The resurrection power to raise Jesus from the dead, raised other people too and they walked back into Jerusalem. Matthew 27:51-53 "At that moment the curtain in the sanctuary of the Temple was torn in two, from top to bottom. The earth shook, the rocks split apart, and tombs opened. **The bodies of many godly men and women who had died were raised from the dead**, **they left the cemetery after Jesus' resurrection, went into the holy city of Jerusalem, and appeared to many people.**"

Many people from the persecuted and underground churches have had similar miracles happen to them and more incredible ones than I have had happen to me. People do get raised from the dead. (People do fake it on TV to get attention. I won't deny there are false preachers and teachers too).

Some people who believe what I believe teach about following "The Way" as it was called in the Bible to follow Jesus, who called himself *The Way, The Truth, and The Life.* People who call themselves "born-again," and "spirit filled" believe what I believe, but not all 'Christians' and not *all* 'born again' believers, believe in the things that I am saying.

The Holy Spirit will network you to other "Believers" who Believe that Jesus is the One and only true Saviour, Lord of all, King of Kings, name above all names and that the Holy Spirit gifts are for today.

He wanted me to go back and re discover. There is a nice verse Jeremiah 6:16 which says 'when you're standing at the crossroads, ask for the ancient ways and ask where the good way is' and I love that version, because it's like He was taking me back to the ancient ways and showing me things that had been replaced – and He is known as The Good Shepherd" and "The Way" and it's like, "ask where the good way is" - so whenever you are following Him or talking to Him, He leads you in that Good Way

JeffMara Podcast Transcript with clarification

The Shepherd's voice

The shepherd calls their sheep with a whistle or a sound, and the sheep come to the shepherd. When you have a pet dog and you call it, it knows the sound of your voice. It comes to you. When a stranger calls, it hesitates. It's not your voice.

In Bible times there were a lot of sheep. Abraham, in the Old Testament, had sheep. David was a shepherd boy before he was a King. Right through to the New Testament there are references to sheep. Non-Christians make fun of Christians calling them "dumb" sheep. I went through a stage of being critical towards Christians thinking of them in this way, so I understand why the "backslidden" and "non-Christians" see and say this.

Sheep are not that dumb. The truth is that being lovingly cared for is special. Being included in God's sheep pen and knowing His voice, personally, is wonderful. You will know His voice. He knows your name.

The Good Shepherd and His Sheep

Verse 10 *(Jesus speaking)* "Very truly I tell you Pharisees, anyone who does not enter the sheep pen by the gate, but climbs in by some other way, is a thief and a robber. ² **The one who enters by the gate is the shepherd of the sheep. ³ The gatekeeper opens the gate for him, and the sheep listen to his voice. He calls his own sheep by name and leads them out.** ⁴ When he has brought out all his own, he goes on ahead of them, and his sheep follow him because they know his voice. ⁵ But they will never follow a stranger; in fact, they will run away from him because they do not recognise a stranger's voice." ⁶ Jesus used this figure of speech, but the Pharisees did not understand what he was telling them.

⁷ Therefore Jesus said again, "Very truly I tell you, **I am the gate for the sheep.** ⁸ All who have come before me are thieves and

robbers, but the sheep have not listened to them. ⁹ **I am the gate**; whoever enters through me will be saved. [a] They will come in and go out and find pasture. ¹⁰ The thief comes only to steal and kill and destroy; I have come that they may have life and have it to the full.

¹¹ **"I am the good shepherd.** The good shepherd lays down his life for the sheep. ¹² The hired hand is not the shepherd and does not own the sheep. So, when he sees the wolf coming, he abandons the sheep and runs away. Then the wolf attacks the flock and scatters it. ¹³ The man runs away because he is a hired hand and cares nothing for the sheep.

¹⁴ **"I am the good shepherd; I know my sheep and my sheep know me—** ¹⁵ just as the Father knows me and I know the Father—and I lay down my life for the sheep. ¹⁶ I have other sheep that are not of this sheep pen. I must bring them also. They too will listen to my voice, and there shall be one flock and one shepherd. ¹⁷ The reason my Father loves me is that I lay down my life—only to take it up again. ¹⁸ No one takes it from me, but I lay it down of my own accord. I have authority to lay it down and authority to take it up again. This command I received from my Father." REF 15

4. THE HARMONY OF THE GOSPELS

The way that I learnt more about who Jesus was, came from the people who lived around the time of Jesus, who wrote about His life: John, Matthew, James (Jacob), and Peter.

The Bible has four different accounts from four different men on the same story, (the life of Jesus) from their perspective; but they weren't all his disciples, in the "original twelve" who were with him. Nevertheless, worth reading and considering. They were Matthew, Mark, Luke, and John.

I can only tell you my story from my perspective. Others may not agree with me, or they may add facts I have skipped out. I have heard a similar analogy to this before and I think it explains the 'perspectives' I'm speaking of:

At a car crash where there is a Doctor and Lawyer and a Mother on the scene, you will get three very different stories.

The Doctor will report casualties and things from a medical perspective.

The Lawyer will look at it through the eyes of 'money' and mentally calculate the cost of the damage.

The Mother will feel the pain of the people involved in the accident, as if it were her own son or daughter involved.

Did you know that is how the Gospels are written? The Gospels are the first four books of the New Testament in the Holy Bible. Matthew, Mark, Luke, John (and the fifth book, Acts, should have been called "Luke Book II" in my opinion and included as it follows on from Luke Book I).

Each man relays his version of 'the life of Jesus' from their perspective. You have for example, Matthew the Tax collector, Luke the Doctor, and John who loves Jesus very much, each giving their version of the same story. To do the story of *The Life of Jesus* justice, one should really do a study of the Gospels in Harmony[16] with each other, (where they overlap); That is why I teach it this way, to whoever comes to do a study with me.

I will point you to the Bible. Even if some say it's full of errors. Read it for yourself. It holds mysteries.

If you think it's just a book. Then read it. If it's *just a book,* what have you got to fear?

I will point you to Jesus.

Ask HIM for YOURSELF if He is real. MATTHEW 7:7 A.S.K. Ask Seek Knock. If you seek Him, you will find Him. **He knows who He is.** If you think *it's just a dead man*. Then ask Him, and you won't get an answer – what have you got to fear?

But if you get an answer – then ... well, then you decide.

5. IMAGINARY FRIEND

The vision that I saw could not be explained away in simple terminology like saying that I saw a "vision." We could not simply say "that was a vision" people who "saw things" were taken into institutions; mental illness had a stigma attached to it. It was far easier to say that I had made it up, that it did not exist, or that it was merely my imagination.

My father concluded that Jesus was my 'imaginary friend' to protect me from the world of critics. To help silence me.

To protect me from ridicule in school. His tactic worked. I never told another soul about it until I wrote my autobiography.

To me, Jesus is not an "imaginary friend." He is not imaginary. He does not "appear" to me or pop in for a "chat." He is not my 'spirit guide' although some would call Him that. I do not see Him on a regular basis appearing in the form that He appeared to me on that day. It has never happened in that way again.

I know that He is real because I *have* seen Him, in that vision and because of a near-death experience that happened twenty years later.

I know that He is real because He delights to bless me daily and encourage me. I will tell you more about it as we go.

I know that He is real because there are historical records of Him being on the earth and many falsified documents created to say things about Him that were not true, because He was seen as a threat. Right from birth He was seen as threat. Herod tried to kill Him before his second birthday.

What is an imaginary friend? It is believed that children who are fearful and traumatised create imaginary friends in their minds to protect themselves.

My childhood was stable. My family was stable.

These 'friends' could be angels/spirits/visions that they have seen, or they could be pretending like imaginative play. Children are creative; a child can put a piece of cardboard in the air, and it is a sword, then put the same cardboard on the mat and it is a boat.

From what I have read, imaginary friends usually disappear when children go to school and the children claim that these 'friends' are not real. They grow out of it.

I have never claimed that this was 'not real' – in fact I have only ever claimed it was, and that He is, very real. He is just as living and real as any person. I have never grown out of it.

> *"The term 'Imaginary friend' has also occasionally been used by atheists to describe the concept of God. Although this tends to offend the religious, it has been suggested that there is a significant similarity between the two concepts.'*[17]

In my opinion, this is partly true in my case. I do not know if my Dad was an atheist because only God truly knows the secrets of a man's heart, but I know that in my conversations with him, he claimed that he was.

> *Atheism, as an explicit position, can be either the affirmation of the non-existence of gods, or the rejection of theism. It is also defined more broadly as an absence of beliefs in deities, or non-theism. Many self-described atheists are sceptical of all supernatural being and cite a lack of empirical evidence for the existence of deities.* [18]

Non-existence of God? If, *"The fool says in his heart, 'There is no God.'"*[19] then my Dad would be called a "fool;" but I do not believe my Dad was a "fool." He was quite a wise and thoughtful person. I do believe that he knew in his heart there was a God, but he was unable to explain 'God' or define Him. Over the course of our lives, he had many conversations with me about God, and about Jesus. I believe that the topic of "God" frustrated my Dad, so he would rather end debates by saying, "man created God" or simply say that Jesus was my "imaginary friend."

> *"Art should comfort the disturbed and disturb the comfortable."*
>
> Cesar A Cruz, Mexican Poet

SANITY IN QUESTION

We Artists are a special breed of people. In my opinion the world did not and does not understand Artists. I'm sure many Artists were considered "mad", "crazy" or "mentally unstable." Maybe I was not a good judge of character of "crazy." Maybe I was one of those "crazy people" and so "crazy creative people" seemed like the "normal" ones to me. In modern day society, now some 30 plus years later, it is not "socially or politically correct" to call someone "crazy." We have an array of other labels. People who saw things were taken into institutions; mental illness had a stigma attached to it.

Likewise, the Mystics were considered the "crazy" ones. I am both an 'artist' and a 'mystic' hence very misunderstood.

When you start seeing angels, you may start to question your sanity. I know that I did question mine. Either He is real, or I am insane. I know the answer for me: I have a sound mind. He is very real.

Many years later after this 'vision' of Jesus, I landed up doing some other "crazy" things, like jumping on an aeroplane to go around the world, by myself, without an airline ticket to the intended destination, Maui Hawaii, and no money to pay for an airline ticket to get there! Let me tell you about that story and the angels that I met along the way, in a minute. First, I will take you through *the years in-between*, from the vision of Jesus until I went to Hawaii nearly twenty years later.

PART 3: MY BACKGROUND

Title: Into the forestPainting by Nathalie de Wet

Interpreting a dream into a painting.

6. INTO THE FOREST

As a young child I was playful. Free. Happy. I was not yet in school. I had not had any religion taught to me or 'in my newsfeed.' I was just young, innocent, and alive to dreaming.

I would dream about this place. It was a forest.

Each night, during this season of this 'recurring dream,' I would go to the same place and walk amongst the trees. I appeared to be a light. I had arms and legs, but it was like I was made of light. Clothed in a white nightie type dress. Modern movies and artists have sometimes depicted ghosts, as see-through, hologram-like beings, that appear to scare people. It was not scary. I was not fearful. In fact, quite the opposite. I was at peace. Blissfully wandering around in the forest. But I looked like a ghost. A white spirit being. A light being, Light-body, or being made of white light.

One night in the forest I was met with hundreds of bubbles. Picture something like when a child blows bubbles into the air for fun. But these bubbles had souls inside them or perhaps they themselves were the Souls. I had tried to reach out and take a hold of them, but they moved away. To me this was indicating that I did not have permission to do that, but also that they were alive or had a mind of their own. That they were living. I say they were "Souls" because that is my understanding of what they were.

Another series of paintings that I did about this forest, were done for my first solo Art exhibition: *Where forests have blue trees.* (Johannesburg, South Africa 1996). I wanted to make it unusual. How do you depict a spiritual place? Paint the trees blue! Nowadays we have the Avatar movie, and it is pretty 'normal' to see creativity on display, but back then, when everyone was painting little realistic scenes, it was slightly dramatic to paint the trees blue.

My favourite of the forest series was a painting of a forest with blue trees, to that I had added some red mushrooms with little white dots. I wanted to make it look like a children's fantasy picture. It was my interpretation of a dream that I didn't want to be questioned on. People would look at it see "fantasy" they could accept it, and not question me. It worked, no one asked questions. They would just see something out of a fantasy book. People who liked fantasy may have imagined fairies, others maybe dragons. I saw my heart longing to be in the forest; *"As the deer pants longingly for the water brooks, so my soul longs for you O God."* so I called the painting "Psalm 42"

The Sovereign LORD is my strength; He makes my feet like the feet of a deer; He enables me to tread on the heights."
Habakkuk 3:19

I kept that one and refused to sell it. I sold all the other paintings. I eventually parted with this original painting because I did not want that piece of artwork to become an idol in my life. It is now with an Art collector in the UK.

7. MY CHURCH HISTORY

We did not go to church. I did not have a religious family background. God was far off.

"*Good God*" was an expression like "*What the f...*" - it had nothing to do with "God" or Him being "Good." The F word was forbidden in our home but using the word *Jesus* in a non-prayerful way was accepted and not reprimanded.

I did not know who Jesus was. This vision of Jesus happened before I knew who Jesus was. Before I'd been told about who He was from a religious viewpoint.

Shortly after the vision, when I was about eight, I went to a school-holiday program run by Methodist Christians. They asked everyone if we wanted to pray "The Sinner's Prayer," (the same as being "born-again") The way they presented it, I thought every little child was going to raise their hand and yell "pick me" but I was wrong. The little girl next to me said "No I'm not going do it." I on the other hand, was keen to "receive Jesus." In my understanding, "I had Jesus" in my heart. I didn't understand that, but that's what the lady said.

I lift my eyes to the mountains. Where does my help come from? My help comes from the Lord, maker of heaven and earth Psalm 121:1

This was the only verse in the Bible that held any significance for me. It was read to us on Veld school in 1984 as I was looking at a mountain. It stuck with me forever. I knew there was a Creator-God. A God far off. I didn't know that Jesus was the Creator-God (according to John chapter 1).

8. WHAT IS BEING 'BORN AGAIN'?

I did not know who started the "born again" Great awakening movement, I thought it was Billy Graham, when I was younger. My understanding on this is that "born again believers" use the verses "You must be born again" John 3:3,6. The point of being 'born again' is the same as "John's baptism of **repentance**" – **a call to repentance** (stopping and turning around) and what the apostles called **"being baptised into the name of Jesus"** - coming to a place of **accepting Jesus** or receiving His name.[21] [22] Another expression of that would be 'calling yourself a "Christian" and having "Christ" as part of your 'identity.'

Most people say a prayer and leave the church "with Jesus" in their back pocket. (Like I did as a little girl at the holiday club, literally written on a piece of paper and shoved into my jeans pocket.) Feeling like they have just signed an insurance policy, *"Well I'm not going to hell now"* - assured of salvation. Some people think they said the prayer – like it's a magic spell or a special formula – and now BAM. SAVED! I don't like calling it "The Salvation prayer" because the prayer doesn't save you. [23]

Another problem is that it lacks **true repentance. True repentance requires HUMILITY.** A heartfelt decision – **a changed life.**

And it lacks **the "Spiritual awakening" (spiritual re-birthing).**

9. WATER BAPTISM

I was about twelve when I requested my parents take me to a church, as I wanted to be water baptised. Somehow, I concluded that I should be water baptised. I don't recall anyone telling me it was something that I was required to do. It wasn't under instruction or compulsion, just something that I desired to do.

My parents did not go to church but used to drop me off and then they told me that if I wanted to continue going, I had to find a lift to church. I got lifts with a kind young man from church who used to pick me up in his little Volkswagen Beetle and bring me home. Around this time, I asked my Mom to read us Bible stories. She read them from a big, illustrated children's Bible that she had sitting on the bookshelf.

(We always had a lot of books in our home. My home now is also full of books. Once my son was taking a selfie and his friend asked on their chat "are you sitting in the library?" – my house is that bad! Or good! Perspective.)

I hung around the Sunday school, *(not church, that was for the "old people")* and Friday night youth group, briefly for about a year or two. After that I spent more time in night clubs with my sisters' acquaintances than I did in a church.

Is "water baptism" required for "Salvation"? No. What is required is HUMILITY. For some people the act of being water Baptised is humbling. For others it is cleansing. (It is not a physical bath, but a decision to wash away behaviours or 'past life' and come into the air out of the water in a form of resurrection to a new way of doing your life.)

I now have a new understanding of "John's water baptism," calling the Jewish people to repentance,[24] compared to what I understood as a twelve-year-old standing in the water being baptised.

I do still believe adult water baptism can be a good thing, if people understand <u>why</u> they are doing it and not doing it under compulsion.

You need Jesus

I had a terrible problem with Christians telling me that I "needed Jesus," because I felt like "I had Him." I was both 'born again' and 'water baptised'. I had different "types" of Christians condemn/judging me as bad for silly reasons; for example, I liked to wear black and black nail polish. I was told by a family member that *I was going to hell* because of that, or that *only people going to hell wore black*. Another time I was friends with a girl at school whose parents banned me from seeing their daughter because I said a swear word. I had said "oh sh!t."

Over the next few years, a lot of Christian people gave me Bibles and told me that I needed Jesus. I was given a NKJV Bible, a Good News Bible, NLT, and a NIV Bible. None of these original books are in my possession any longer. And since then (mid 80's) I have had many more Bibles in my possession and released them.

Nobody took the time to walk me through some basic steps after 'saying the little prayer'. Until one day, a young girl, took many hours to answer my questions and teach me how she would use a journal.

Journaling was a huge key for me in the journey of processing my pain. The cover of *'Discovering an Artist'* is a painting that I did of books, to represent 'a pile of journals.'

Unlikely friends

The place that I learnt the most about "hearing from God" was through my journals and reading a Bible; hours of prayer and listening to worship music while I painted. Not through a church. Not through organised religion. To coin a phrase, it was "through doing carpet time."

Miracles. Supernatural miracles. Miracle healings. Supernatural provision. All these things were learnt through practical demonstration and application of the scriptures I was reading. **Taking God's word literally and doing what it said.** A principal I had learnt while in school, when TJ introduced me to journalling, her church and some little books on "faith."

In Highschool I had an Art class-friend. The teacher had the tables arranged in groups with 4 people sitting together. I was a spare leg, a loner. I landed up with her and her friends, a group of kind churchy Christians. I doubt we would have ever become good friends if God did not arrange that. Back then TJ was very involved with her church. I was very involved in going to night clubs and parties.

She would often invite me, but I would mostly decline the invitations and land up going out with my sister and sister's friends to a nightclub. (Yes, I was underage, and there was a lot of unsavoury stuff going on.)

I thought initially that this church was 'weird'. The first time I recall being in a meeting was a prayer meeting at her house.

They called these mid-week 'home groups.' We were standing in the garden and these people were all praying over each other. People were *standing* and praying *over each other*. Putting their *hands* on each other. If that wasn't already freaking my brain out, they prayed out *aloud!* In the Baptist church everyone bowed their heads and spoke to themselves or God in their head. (Excuse the pun). And they were *Praying in tongues.* I was backing away thinking "Don't touch me!" I think they saw my comical expressions. No one touched me.

One night I recall going to TJ's Friday night youth group. I'm sure it must have been the first time that I went to the youth meeting. This was a meeting where they all met together in a hall, not a home group. The whole bunch of youth (over 200 people) called themselves "Frontline Youth." They had T-shirts. Loud music. And no entertainment. There were no Friday night games and activities, potluck, and Pollyanna. All they wanted to do was pray. For hours!

The first thing that struck me was there was no *Sunday smile*. People were like family. It was a very 'huggy' church; everyone hugged each other when you arrived. (I liked that they didn't kiss. The Bible says, 'greet each other with a holy kiss'. I'm good thanks, but a hug is fine – or a side hug if I'm a little uncomfortable).

The next thing that struck me was how it sounded when

the whole bunch of youth (over 200 people) sang in tongues and spontaneously stopped. It was INSTANT. The entire room stopped. There was no music conductor at the time. It was like a full stop in the spirit realm.

How can you have such 'crowd control' and call the Spirit-filled /Pentecostal/Charismatic churches: chaotic? God is very organised.

My conclusion now, is that the Holy Spirit is very organised. Man's idea of "organised." is not God's idea. When the Holy Spirit takes over a meeting, it doesn't make sense to man. It doesn't look good on social media or camera. Spiritual things like 'speaking in tongues' look weird. When God takes over a meeting it is usually uncomfortable for our 'flesh' because it deals with our sin and our pride. It makes perfect sense afterwards. We come to a place of being wrecked for the ordinary. We don't want ordinary. We want more of God in our lives.

God had never really answered my prayers up until then. I had probably never really prayed. I received a little 'book of prayers' from a Great Aunt with rhymes to recite over meals, but we never did that. We never said "Grace" at meals. And there was that Holiday Club where we said a "repeat after me" type prayer.

That night at the youth group, the minister spoke about running your race with focus. Eyes fixed. No distractions. His message was about *"Keeping our eyes fixed on Jesus."* 25

Some things changed drastically for me that night. *(I wrote them in my other book).*

Eventually, what probably *really* caught my attention was a little book that TJ let me read. I avoided reading, (I was not very good at reading). This booklet was only a few pages. I don't recall, maybe 80 pages? It was written by a teenager about his spiritual experience. "I saw Heaven" by Roberts Liardon. After I read it, she was saying something like, "Isn't that amazing?" I was thinking, "Maybe she won't think I'm crazy if I tell her about seeing Jesus and going into the forest…." Dr. Roberts Liardon had reassured me that day of my sanity as I learnt that I was not the only one who has seen 'heaven' stuff. I remained quiet and said nothing about the joy exploding and bouncing inside of me, and simply said, "Yes it's interesting," nonchalantly. I decided to completely stop going out with my sister to nightclubs and rather commit myself to the young adult group. This church just upped its' level piquing my interest.

The Trinity

Another reason why I had thought that TJ's church was 'weird' because what I perceived was that this church spoke out aloud to the "deities." They spoke to the Holy Spirit, the Father, and the Son. They explained the three were "one" but **separate** and addressed them separately.

Do I believe this now?

*"Jesus replied, "This is the most important: 'Hear O Israel, the Lord our God, **the Lord is One."** Mark 12:29 Cf Deut 6:4 "You believe that **God is one**. Good for you! Even the demons believe that-and shudder." James 2:19*

I was learning more about God's IDENTITY – the names given. In the Trinitarian language of the Bible, the Bible reveals The Father is God, The Holy Spirit is God, and The Son is God, in human, flesh form. Triune God. The concept was strange for me.

In the brief season that I attended a Baptist church, they had only addressed God as the *Heavenly Father*. One God who had sent his Son to earth. I understood that His son was like a demigod, the Father seemed to be the main "God" guy. We got a new Sunday school teacher who used to pray to Jesus. I asked her, *"is it ok for us to talk to Jesus?"* I had seen Jesus. My Spirit knew He was Jesus, but I had never *talked* to him! My brain thought that concept would be weird. It would be like I was talking to a ghost.

I recall the first time I got some courage to speak to Jesus when I was sixteen; the first time I attended TJ's Friday night youth group meeting. I came home and prayed. He answered.

The story is in my other book, under the chapter LOOKING UP AT THE BANNER.

In my life, it was very significant to **receive the Holy Spirit** *as well as* the **Father** and the **Son**.

10. BAPTISM IN THE HOLY SPIRIT

Spiritual Awakening and Meeting Ruach Ha Kodesh

In my last year of high-school, around seventeen years old, I began attending my school friends' church. She had been inviting me for about two years before I finally gave in, stopped going to night clubs and went to her church and youth group instead.

After some time, I went back to the Baptist Church's minister where I'd been water baptised, at my request, and asked him why that church never spoke about the Holy Spirit. I asked why they claimed to believe in 'the Trinity' and only spoke to the Father and of the Son. I was told "we are afraid of the power" as the answer. I was not satisfied with that so, I asked the Holy Spirit to show me who He was.

So, The Holy Spirit did. With that, I was 'Baptised with the Holy Spirit' and spoke in tongues as the apostles were in the Book of Acts.

The first book I read on the topic of *speaking to the Holy Spirit* was, "Good morning Holy Spirit" by Benny Hinn.[26] It was mind bending, in an interesting way. Some teach it is heresy. He-She is *with us now*, so I understand the concept of talking to the Holy Spirit.

If someone tells me "you can't read that!" - then I go and read it to find out why not! I've been told by some that's "courageous and bold" and by others "that's stupid and irresponsible." In my opinion, in this age of information, it's irresponsible to be uninformed.

Before *amazing* things happened, over the years ahead, one simple thing happened first: *I wanted to read the Bible.*

I did not read. My Mom helped me with school book-reviews. I hated reading! This was indeed very significant. We are not talking about a 30-page booklet,[27] we are talking about a thick book made up of many books! The Bible has History, poetry, drama, letters and more.

For the first time ever, when I read the Bible, *I wasn't bored.* I was so excited it was like words jumped off the page into my spirit. I felt charged and alive. I was so excited about this experience I wanted to tell everyone.

I irritated everyone! At school I was labelled and teased

but I didn't care. I was so excited about seeing things with new eyes (and ears)

Deafness

I struggled to read. I was born with a bit of deafness in my ear. I struggled to comprehend sounds; when I was young, my family joke was, I used to say "dem des" instead of "then there is" because that's what I was hearing.

Deafness healed

In high school I used to tell everybody, "I believe in miracles" and the reason for that, was because my hearing was healed when I received the "Baptism of the Holy Spirit." I could hear. My hearing was restored.

I could hear which meant I could understand language better and I was so excited about reading. When I read the Bible, it was alive and it was like, it was, a spiritual book and it was feeding my spirit. I was really excited about it. I became what people would call, 'a fanatic' or 'Jesus' freak' or whatever; but I wasn't really, I was just so excited for the miracle of being able to hear!

I used to say, "I believe in miracles" a little friend at school was ridiculing me and she gave me a little (paper) badge and it said, "I believe in miracles" and they were (playfully) mocking me. I got a badge, - (I got one from the Christian bookshop, Kathryn Kuhlmann said "I believe in miracles") and I wore it with pride, "yes, I do!" I'm healed and really excited about that!

(In a YouTube video about my hearing miracle, I also mention another healing miracle that took place after I had experienced some trauma to my head. Ben Hughes, Pour it out ministries, prayed for me on the Sunshine coast, Australia in about 2019.)

A DIFFERENT KIND OF SPIRITUAL AWAKENING

If ever you have heard of a yoga 'Spiritual awakening', you may know what I am speaking of when I say I had a "Spiritual Transformation Experience" or a "Spiritual awakening experience" when I was Baptised with the Holy Spirit. Unlike the Kundalini (The Serpent Spirit), The Holy Spirit, Ruach Ha Kodesh, (The Spirit of Holiness) is characterised by The Gifts of The Holy Spirit.

There are nine gifts, one of the nine being the "working of

miracles." These became "my normal." Seeing daily miracles. Believing for them. Being teased because I said, "*I believe in miracles*." I honestly could write another entire book on all the incredible things I've lived through over my short lifetime! I will mention many of them in this book as we go, but there are more I have not detailed: Believing for arms and legs to grow and they grew. Keys fitting doors they weren't made for. The needle moving up on the fuel tank. Seeing incredible things in the Spiritual realm. Being woken by Angels and told I needed to get up and pray. It's glorious to live in this daily! So much fun to be obedient to God and watch what He can do and does do. *It's literally out of this world*. But it requires that we do our part. OBEDIENCE. You need to DO WHATEVER HE TELLS YOU TO DO.[22] Like getting up to pray when you would rather sleep. Sometimes you may not like what you need to do, and others may not like what you do. There is always a reason. DO IT SCARED and DO IT ANYWAY.

Art and creativity encouraged

After I "met the Holy Spirit" I began attending TJ's church more and then exclusively, for a season. I want to say, "I left the Baptist Church well," but the truth is, I did something very naughty.

In TJ's church I met many interesting Arty people. They had some 'interesting looking people' attend their meetings and me wearing black was not offensive or an issue. Creativity was accepted. I felt accepted, not judged.

Even though I felt a measure of love and kindness at the 'traditional/fundamental' type of churches; it was what I called "the Sunday smile." I'd always felt like I was being judged. Looked at down someone's nose.

In this new church, it was easy to bring people in off the street and so we did. We would find homeless people and bring them to church. Then introduce them to someone so that they could turn their lives around. You didn't need to wear "your Sunday best."

We were all there to worship God. It was *all* about worshipping HIM. All about praying. For hours. We would sit and weep on our knees or stand or clap or dance. It wasn't about us. *It was all about Him.*

I wanted to do something for God, but I didn't know what.

The Baptist Church were always looking for women to

serve the tea and babysit the children. That was all that the women were good for pretty much; and maybe arranging flowers or playing the organ but those were usually appointed jobs.

I committed myself to becoming a Sunday school teacher at the Baptist church for one year. Went through a week of training under the supervisor and started the next week with a classroom 'full' of gorgeous little girls. We had so much fun. This "Baptism of the Holy Spirit" thing was so good! I couldn't believe that the Baptist church was so dead to it. I wrestled with it a lot. During the classroom time I had tried to give them as much teaching on it from the Bible as I could in between the 'dead' lessons. I was just learning about it myself, so it was more the Holy Spirit teaching them than me.

Then one day I decided forget these rules and boundaries. *(I know that sounds like rebellion. It was more like escaping prison. Freedom.)* I took my classroom of four little girls into the toilet *(I know it's awful. Today there is no way I would have done this!)* I had told them, 'we are going to pray for the Baptism of the Holy Spirit, but I will get into trouble if I do this in the classroom'. The classrooms had little wooden dividers and I was sure that the praying in tongues would create a negative reaction from a neighbouring teacher. What I know now is that the Holy Spirit could have sound-proofed the room or done something supernatural.

The Holy Spirit was gracious, and the girls were Baptised in the Holy Spirit and spoke in tongues. We left the toilet and went back to class.

I remained their teacher until the end of the year and those four young girls came every single week. They loved me and I adored them. At the end of the year, I presented them with small black hardcovered Bibles. The girls made me cards and I took a photo of the little ladies with their Bibles. I still have the cards they made for me and the photo.

I knew that I couldn't stay at this church any longer. I wanted to be in a church that wasn't dead, and that was moving in faith and miracles and where I could freely pray in tongues.

11. CATCH THE FIRE

When I turned twenty-one, I enrolled in night Bible-school held through TJ's church. I studied there for about two or three years. We mostly read the Holy Bible, using a Strong concordance and Vines Bible dictionary. Studying the Bible inductively. The Bible was our textbook. We had one textbook called "Christian foundations"[28] but we hardly referred to it.

Years after I was Baptised with The Holy Spirit, and around the time I ended my studies at the Bible college, the church became involved with a church in Toronto, Canada.[29] The church called their meetings "Catch the Fire" *(now known as "The Toronto Blessing")*

This movement was dynamic. People humbled and genuinely worshipping the One and only God, The Miracle worker. "Humility" is the best word I can think of to describe it. Church auditorium was an atmosphere of miracles. Many *unusual* things began to take place. The worship was incredible!

I landed up singing on stage as part of the "worship team"

leading the worship songs. It became normal to see the spiritual things taking place. Like gold dust falling on the people and other *physical manifestations*. Demons leaving people, healing miracles and unusual stuff like that for us – normal stuff for God.

People praying for days on end and …just praying. Fasting to pray, was normal. Skipping movies and other secular events with friends, to rather come to church and pray every night, was normal. Praying for 5 hours was normal.

'Falling down' (also called "being slain in the Spirit") was normal. *It is mentioned in the Bible many times.*

My first experience of being slain happened to me in 1990. I didn't believe it was "of God" at the time, and I was questioning things. One night the group were praying, and I recall thinking, 'God is not going to knock me over' and in an instant I was laying on my back on the ground. He showed me it was most definitely Him and He knew exactly what He was doing - and that He wasn't going to be taking orders from me! I was not scared or hurt, just flabbergasted that He could do that so seamlessly.

As 'Catch the Fire' meetings went on, for weeks, people

would crawl into the building because the power of God was so strong that standing became impossible at times.

There were other things that happened.

One thing that transpired was that my husband-to-be had moved to Johannesburg a few years prior. He was invited to one of these "Catch the Fire" meetings. We never met that day, but I would not be surprised if I was singing on stage that very time that he visited, because I faithfully sang every single day, for weeks as the meetings kept rolling on. He thought we were all weird.

Another was that the movement came under huge criticism from many. These Holy Spirit manifestations came with shaking, jerking, rolling on the floor and a fire like heat sensation in the body. People said it was not the Holy Spirit, but a Hindu tradition known as "Kundalini awakening." The two are very different. As I've already said Kundalini is linked to "The Serpent spirit." (In the Bible there are things recorded which are linked to the Serpent Spirit.) The Holy Spirit baptism also known as, being "filled with the Holy Spirit" or "spirit filled," is linked to the "Ruach Ha Kodesh" the "Spirit of Holiness" or the Holy

Spirit – some people call Him, The Holy Ghost.

The serpent has always been the deceiver. The serpent always tries to mimic God and be God. God does it first! Satan is the liar. It's not the other way around.

Discovering and Artist extract

How fantastic for the serpent if Christians' fight against each other. A house divided against itself cannot stand. Imagine if every Christian received miracle working power from the Holy Spirit and lived an 'abundant life In Jesus'? Imagine if every Christian believed that Healing was for today and they didn't <u>need</u> to be sick. Imagine every Christian was living in divine health and believed God at His Word, when He said, 'by his stripes we WERE healed'. (If we 'were', then we are).

Some people think they are *being wise to be critical;* They would say the new ministries are false, with false teachers and false prophets. In some cases, I absolutely agree with their conclusions based on the 'fruit'. We need to be wise and watchful. There are 'weeds amongst the wheat'. It's *not our job* to pull up the weeds. God will send His Angels to sort that out because we are human. Did you get that –

it's not our job! I feel that we need to be careful about being judgemental and critical. We need to *be watchful* and choose carefully.

Catch the Fire/Toronto Blessing came with manifestations of gold dust in the meetings. In some meetings around the world there were precious gemstones and oil pouring from the pores of people's hands. We experienced the gold dust regularly.

12. THE GOLD DUST STORIES

I know some people want to know more about the gold dust manifestation! Some people have never experienced it, whereas others, like Ruth Ward Heflin, said that she had experienced it in revival meetings [30] in the 60's, 70's and 80's.

Did it fall from the ceiling? No, it did not for us, but I have heard that in some churches it did. I have read naysayers saying it was put in the aircon system of churches. Look, maybe there was some church somewhere that was so desperate to pretend they had it, that they put glitter in the aircon, but the gold came through the pores of your being and looked like glittering gold eyeshadow, but it didn't wipe off. It was like gold dust appearing on our hands and making our faces shine. I'm talking about gold dust appearing like sweat, not being pumped into the room, or falling from the ceiling.

The supernatural oil came through the pores of your skin.

It was supernatural.

Later in 1998, I was in Israel. I had experienced the Gold dust some years before at our church's 'Catch the Fire' meetings, but just before I left Israel, I was staying at the last place I stayed at in Israel. They had a guest speaker, and they experienced the gold dust for the first time. I shared that story in my other book.

Another Gold dust story

In 2019 I painted live at a prophetic Ignite meeting, the picture is called *'Angels shifting atmospheres.'* When I came home, I placed the painting on my easel. It had gold dust on it. I let it sit there for a few days admiring the gold dust until it faded and then I passed it on to its new owner. It was the first painting I've done that had gold dust appearing on it.

The gold dust still happens to me sometimes when I pray for people.

This list of things in this book is by no means fully comprehensive of all the things I began to see hear and experience in this "weird" church. *Not weird at all to God!*

While I was catching gold dust

My husband-to-be was the last intake of the compulsory conscription.

For many years of South Africa's history, all young men who left school were expected to do two years of compulsory, conscription military training. At eighteen they were shipped out to the borders of the country. Trained to fire a rifle and kill people.

All young men left school and went straight off into the army. Those who did not, were seen as "weak." Those who went through it, came out "mature" (damaged). Some very traumatised by the horrors they had seen. Some never came out, like our friends, who died, far away from the comforts of their family and homes.

Some of the young men struggled to adapt to the norms of society and either remained in the army or went to join the Police force or civilian security companies; or landed up becoming heavy drinkers or using substances. Not all.

Young men were trained to believe that *the terrorists were bad*. The enemy. When the terrorists (ANC) they had been fighting against, became the leaders of the country, many of the young men who had once fought on the borders, now older with families, decided to leave the country.

We both grew up in the Old South Africa under "apartheid" and through the transition placing the country under the ANC government under the leadership of the world renown Mr Nelson Mandela. Madiba, they called him. 'The New South Africa.' The country went through many changes. Everything was renamed and the flag was changed. The country was divided into new sections and Afrikaans men were removed from their jobs and replaced with untrained black women. They called it Black empowerment.

Change. Adapt. Change. Adapt. Change. Adapt.

Some could not accept the changes. Some could not adapt. Anyone who left was considered a 'traitor' by those who would never leave.

13. PERSPECTIVE

New knowledge is a powerful thing. It affects our perceptions of things and changes our perceptions, or may I be Arty and say Perspectives? It is all about PERSPECTIVE!

I can only tell you my story, from my perspective, as truthfully as I can. My perspective came from an 'encounter' experience. I wasn't trained in all kinds of knowledge and sciences. It was a personal perspective. A relationship perspective.

I knew that Jesus was kind. I knew that He oozed with love. I knew that He was for me not against me. I knew he was able to transcend matter. I knew He had his body; he was alive in His body. All those stories that said anything contrary, I could easily dismiss as fables and rumours.

If people said he was a violent person, I could dismiss that too. He was love incarnate!

Maybe, he was a zealot. Zeal consumed him. Maybe historically he did carry a sword (Peter obviously had a sword to cut off the soldiers' ear). Maybe He was Yeshua Zebaoth, The Wolf. I did not see Him as a violent man. Yet

I did see Him as strong.

Yeshua Emmanuel. Seen by others as 'son of the household of Joseph.' Mary was the mother of his Body.

My perspective was formed through the eyes of innocence. I did not experience any more open visions of Him coming and standing in my bedroom. One encounter changed my life.

To me, by my 'coming to know Jesus', I am talking about a Person – not about my "higher self" or consciousness or the "Christ consciousness." A person. Someone who walked the earth then left. I believe that He rose from the dead in His physical body, and he is in a place outside of our known physical world. I know about 'the stolen body theory' (that his body was stolen out of the grave and that he didn't rise from the dead) It's not stolen. He has it. He doesn't appear in bodily form to anyone. He tells us He won't do that, and when He does return, which He will, we will all see Him.

He does appear in visions. He appeared to me as He appeared to John in the Book of Revelation and as He has appeared to many people since John. This is not the verses about deceptions in Matthew 24. These are visions. Visions are for the last days. The Prophet Joel said there will be an increase of dreams and visions in the last days.

As an Artist I have learnt how to create optical illusions, 3-dimensional objects on a flat surface like a canvas, or a *Trompe L'oeil* wall mural which 'tricks the eye'. "Seeing Jesus" was not an optical illusion.

He is for EVERYONE who would believe. I don't like the assumption that "Jesus is only the *Christian deity.*"

He is The Light.[31] Anyone can see and experience The Light who is willing. Jesus doesn't care what religion you are. He is still The Light.[31] This Light is such a difficult concept to explain to people who are in the darkness. It is more than a mere white light. It is more than "enlightenment" but it is all of those things as well.

I know that I will be 'celebrated' by people who resonate with me. We go where we are celebrated, not where we are tolerated and hated. People with similar gifts to me, resonate with me. People who have experienced the rejection of Protest-ant churches who 'protest' everything that doesn't suit their dogma and call us "backslidden

Christians" because we decided to question the things we were being told.

Maybe you are like a young girl I met in Israel who said to me on the bus at the Dead Sea, *"I want this Jesus who keeps helping you,"* and you're wondering how do YOU find Him.

First, look up. Do you remember when I heard the voice as a little girl in Chapter 1 saying, "The only way out is up."? I looked up. When I was in Amsterdam and I didn't know where to go, I looked up to heaven to cry out to God and I saw the sign on the top of a building. **Sometimes the first step is taking our eyes off ourselves, and our situation and looking up. Look to Him.** When Moses was in the desert, and they had no water the people were grumbling and complaining, and I am sure it was not pleasant for him to be both thirsty and have all these people complaining to him. He cried out to the Lord and the Lord gave him the solution. Cry out to God.

It is my hope that you will walk outside, if you can, and look up and talk to Him. And if you can't go outside or lift your head to heaven – you can still LOOK UP in your heart.

Take your focus off yourself and your issues and look up.

We have a free will

I shared previously a lesson I went through on "free will" when I came to understand that humans have free will. *(You can find that illustration explained in my other book in the section under Memphis, TN.)*

On earth we get to choose to accept or reject Jesus. We can choose to be close to Jesus – we choose to stop our busy lives and include Him in our lives. Or we choose to not do that. We have a free will; we are not forced to choose Him.

We choose to accept Jesus dying on the cross as our substitute or not. It's our choice. We are presented with information from various angles, and we are given a choice about what we will choose to believe. You cannot say Muhammed, The Holy Qur'an or anyone else, *(because Muhammed did not actually write it),* told me not to believe it. It is your choice to believe or not. It is your choice to question what you are told or to not question.

Jesus will say to you *personally,* "WHO DO YOU SAY I AM?" and you must answer Him.

PART 4: ANGELIC BEINGS IN THE LIGHT

Title: Angels shifting atmospheres   Painting by Nathalie de Wet

14. ANGELS ON THE CEILING

In an atmosphere of worship, you see angels.

One of the beautiful open visions that I had, happened in church during the time that the music plays and people sing worship songs to God.

We were just worshipping, (singing songs) when He showed me what was going on in spiritual realm. There were angels all around the ceiling. They were worshipping Him. Their wings are making music and their voices. There was this 'sparkle dust' coming from their wings as they were singing. I called it "sparkled dust" because what do you call something that doesn't have a name in English? It's not like everyone is walking around seeing angels worshipping Jesus, but one day we will see it. Then you will know. You will say "aah there's the sparkle dust!"

It was sparkly and it looked like dust. This sparkle dust reminds me of when you see dust particles moving in the air in the rays of light. This dust was shiny. Shimmering white like the glory of God. Sparkling like diamonds sparkle. If you can imagine dust being alive and being a type of substance floating upward and gathering on the ceiling. It was collecting in the ceiling by not in the ceiling, ...that same thing about the Jesus vision right at the beginning, where I explained that the spiritual transcends the natural but it's still tangible. It's like in the natural, but it's not in the natural. Like another realm, two realms at once.

It was there gathering on the ceiling of this church building. Then in the natural you could see this cloud coming down over the people... I don't know maybe some people could not to see it, I don't know, I could see that. It was a cloud in the church, like a water vapour cloud, but it was a glory cloud not a rain cloud. When you worship Him and the atmosphere becomes "thick" with the glory, you get the glory cloud, I think. I think worship creates a "substance" in the atmosphere which I'll call "sparkle dust" until the day I die; then I'll go and have a chat with the angels, they can tell me what it really is and explain all the many things that I do not understand.

What did the angels look like?

In my excitement to rush through my experiences I forgot to tell people what they looked like, almost assuming that everybody knew what angels look like. I'd seen them a few times and it had become normal. Sometimes I forget that my normal isn't everybody's normal. There was a stage that I asked God to stop letting me see them, but now I'd like to see them more often.

I explained the appearances of the "people ones" that I saw (shapeshifted). You get different angels, and they look different. The "normal" ones that we see, look like people. They interact with us. Walk amongst us. Talk to us. I can tell you that they are solid beings. They aren't a ghostly mist or see-through. They are actual beings. They look like people. The Bible says you could be entertaining angels and you don't know at the time that they are angels. You realise in retrospect.

They are not people. People have 'spirits' and you may have heard people referring to their 'spirit' as 'angels' or saying people 'become angels,' but people are people and angels are angels. Angels can "shapeshift" into human form. Walk amongst us. Eat food. But people and angels are two different things.

Then you have the ones that appear as a ghost, not see

through, a solid being. They are quite beautiful. They have this calmness, peacefulness, serenity about them. They aren't in a rush or urgently frantic. They move with lightning speed when there is something to do, but without fear and panic.

Once when I was painting a wall mural God said, "WHY DO YOU PAINT THEM TO LOOK LIKE HUMANS?" And immediately I realized, "yes, they are not human!" Traditionally angels have been painted to look humans with wings, but He wanted me to paint them to look like angels, Spiritual beings. They don't all have wings, or if they do, I don't always see the wings. Some just look like they have arms and legs and bodies. They move and float around with weightless effort. They aren't little cherubs that buzz around. They are about 6-7ft tall. They are big, strong, gentle giants.

You have one assigned to you for life. I call that "the one assigned" to me. Some people say that's your Guardian angel. They serve God cheerfully. They love us. I love that they hang around because they want to.

Sometimes God assigns more to you. If they don't like you,

they still hang around because God told them to. They listen to Him and do whatever He tells them to do. God may send them to assist you and then they can leave when you complete the task or they can choose to leave, if you decide to stop doing something that God has told you to do. They are gentle. They don't force you to do anything. They might nudge you, but if you don't take the hint they can leave and go help someone else. They are always busy. They love to serve God.

If you tell them to do something that God didn't authorise, they won't listen to you. They answer to Him. They get their instructions from Him, not you.

Glory clouds

This cloud came down over the people in the worship. Years later I heard people speaking about "the glory clouds." I started understanding that this first vision that I had, the shining light around him, was his glory, and in time I would call it the *"Shekinah* glory" or "the visible glory of God." These glory clouds are His visible, to the naked eye, glory.

Jesus' feet

Once when I was slain in the spirit, I saw feet standing next to me but then I realised that the feet were in the spiritual realm, not the natural realm, that it was like an open vision. And then I realised who they belonged to.

Jesus' laugh

Of all my experiences with Jesus, one thing that was very special to me, that stuck out to me about Jesus, was His joy and his love-laughter. He has got a deep laugh. When He laughs you want to laugh with Him. You are filled with joy. He oozes with joy and love.

Piece of the cross

I had many times of being "caught up in the spirit." Like seeing visions or experiences the lower level 'impressions.' This day I was 'slain in the spirit' or 'lying down on the ground' and I saw a piece of wood (this was an open vision – it was very clear in front of me.)

It was really rough. It was about 10 centimetres by 2 centimetres. As I was looking at this piece of wood I was thinking, "what are you trying to show me?" "is this my heart?" "have I got like such a hard heart?" and I didn't know what it was. I was looking at it. It was really rough, like not sandpapered, it was terrible. Like it had splints of wood.

Then he said to me, "this is a piece of wood from my cross"

I burst out crying because I was suddenly overwhelmed, "whoa... that was sticking into your back!" That's not nice.

I had been really obsessed with understanding the crucifixion. I couldn't understand it. I didn't understand it and why did he have to be crucified? One day I had said to him, "You know that I really want to understand the crucifixion more." I wanted to be at the crucifixion. To go back in time and witness it, if such a thing was possible.

After I realized what it was and cried, He explained, "you can't handle 10 centimetres of my cross. You're not going to be able to handle seeing and understanding the crucifixion."

I accepted that. That vision was enough information. I didn't need to know any more about the crucifixion.

This was before "The Passion movie" and obviously "The Passion movie" gives us a much clearer understanding of the reality of the cross, but at that point, the only thing I'd seen about the cross was these little statues in churches, which make him look anaemic and skinny.

But I hadn't really recognised his pain and when I did, I cried.

Jesus sounds like … thunder

What did Jesus sound like? When He did speak to me, He's got a male voice, obviously. He speaks with very few words. He's not like me who talks too much. If you think of the commander of an army or military person, he's like that. he's very direct. He is a commander; He speaks but he speaks like a command. When he said to me that I could come back into my body he said, "OK, BUT IT WILL BE A STRUGGLE." He told me so I knew what to expect, but he was direct and to the point.

When He speaks, He doesn't need a lot of words for you to understand what He is saying. He speaks very few words, but you know exactly what He's saying.

Leaving the 'weird' church

Around this time, I also ended up leaving TJ's church. It

was a natural progression. I removed myself from the worship team. Over the next two years, I headed off overseas for a few months at a time. When I left for good it was because I had signed up to a missionary training course in Hawaii. While I was away, the church closed.

It's odd how I always thought of it as "her church" or "Doug's church" (Senior Pastor) but I never thought of it as "My church." If I spoke about "my church" I would be talking about the Baptist church where I had been water baptised; even although I never went into membership at the Baptist church.

There was a shift in the local church. From my perspective: *I felt like the wave of God swept over the church to wash it clean, but then church tried to hang onto it and 'own' it.* **You cannot own a move of God.**

It seemed to me that some people started doing things **out of themselves**. Acting. It became 'about the movement' and publicity, and not about humility. Others from other churches were coming to make fun of the Christians and the movement, as it gained publicity. It became a bit of a spectacle.

When I left South Africa I thought that I was going off "to save the world." *(Because I didn't realise that had already been done by Jesus, dying on the cross).* I had a vague idea of wanting to help people. It was my hope to complete the first part of the missionary training on the course in America then go to Bali Indonesia on a mission's trip (SOM) then I had planned to move on to their next course (DTS). What I signed up for, wasn't yet their foundational course (DTS) to getting into their programmes. I believed God had pointed out "that part of the world" (Indonesia, the Ring of fire islands, Eastern side of Australia, New Zealand, Tasmania). Hawaii was somehow the first big step. **I thought that my husband must be there waiting for me.** *("That part of the world" is where I am living now, many years later.)*

I had *no clear direction*. My head and heart were all over the place! Sometimes, we go *through* stuff, to figure out what we are not. On my travels as a missionary, I began to discover that I was not a missionary. I had to go *through this* journey to discover that I was not a missionary. God did not *require* that I become a missionary. I thought that He did. He understood that I was created to PAINT! *But I didn't know that. It became clear to me when I was sitting in Amsterdam's Red-Light district. The story is relayed in my autobiography of how I went from Missionary to Artist.*

I worked as a missionary, alongside three ministries and under two different churches over the course of several years. One told me they didn't support the other one, because it wasn't "their programme." Another told me they would place my photo on the church notice board to remind people to pray; when I returned three months later, it was gone. I don't know how many weeks it was up, or if they even put it up, to be completely honest. Maybe your church is different.

When you leave, they wave goodbye with a *"God bless you"* Truth is, most missionaries out on the "field" don't have much support or prayer cover. Your mother prays, and my Grandmother prayed. Everyone else forgets about you and continues with their own lives, family, commitments. I sent out a letter to remind people of my existence *(in those days, sending out letters by snail-mail cost a lot of money it became too expensive)*. Usually no one replied. Churches offered no tangible "down to earth" support, and maybe not even a letter or email in reply to your updates. They may tell you later, they were happy that you wrote. *(You provided some light reading entertainment for them, free of charge.)* I did not agree with the way ministry organisations worked and the lack of "natural" support missionaries had. Missionaries had to trust God for their "supernatural" provision, and pretty much hope that back home people were praying for them. Meanwhile they were often facing dire situations and when they returned home, like military veterans, they have PTSD from traumas they have faced and feel like 'civilians' cannot relate to them. Some end up not wanting to return to civilian way of life. It's like a prisoner preferring life in prison.

15. GOING TO HAWAII

(Extracts from *Discovering an Artist* Chapter 10 United States of America are included in this section)

The Lord was talking to me about going to Hawaii. As a South African going to Hawaii was hard to comprehend because of exchange rates.

I was passionate about doing what God told me to do. I said, "OK I'll go to Hawaii." I'd go on a missionary training course with this organisation called YWAM, (youth with a mission). I enrolled and signed myself onto their mission training course.

I was accepted as expected but I still bounced around with joy when I got the acceptance letter! It would all be happening the following year in June, a little over 6 months away. I didn't have a clue how I was going to pay for it.

I tried intently to save up as much as I could for my pending trip to Hawaii. I did everything in "my own strength" (the Bible calls it) to get enough money to get on this course. What a logical person would do, pay for the course.

The original "muffin lady" at work handed me her recipe. I started baking muffins every single morning before work. I was driving my father crazy with the mess in the kitchen that I would rush out the door in the mornings, leaving the clean-up for the evenings when I returned from work. Each morning I'd wrap the muffins in plastic cling-wrap, take them to work and sell them. People would come past my desk and buy them fresh, daily. I became known as "The Muffin Lady," some people didn't even know my name!

No matter how hard I tried, I didn't get enough to pay for the course that I had enrolled myself into. At which point people began telling me I was "crazy" and "insane," "a nut," for thinking of leaving a perfectly good job and travelling across the world, to literally the other side, alone, without any money. They didn't even know the half of it! I still did not have enough money to buy the aeroplane ticket and I did not own my own suitcase either.

> *My God shall supply all your needs according to His riches in glory by Christ Jesus Philippians 4:19 NKJV*

Trust God for provisions

God said to me, "I WANT YOU TO TRUST ME FOR THE

PROVISIONS" and "I don't want you to buy toothpaste" and so I didn't buy any. Each day as the toothpaste was getting closer to an end, and I was getting more anxious.

I was also fearful that maybe I was actually insane. I was swaying between packing up and not sure if I should. I had faith, but then I doubted. Double-mindedness* had kept me "unstable." (*"A double minded man is unstable in all his ways" James 1:8)

On the last day I said, *"OK I'm going to buy toothpaste today because you haven't provided."* I was working in an advertising company. I was one of the senior secretaries. I arrived at work and sitting on my desk was a gift pack - six tubes of Colgate toothpaste! We had signed on Colgate on as a new client, and they had given each senior staff member a gift bundle. I laughed out loudly! The lesson I learnt: GOD IS NEVER LATE! He is always right one time!

Angels among us

Another day I went to work and went on my lunch break. Across the road from the building that I worked in, was a shopping centre. There was a grocery food shop within the shopping centre, it was called Checkers. When you came out of Checkers there was this huge open, an entrance way, that was a walkway. Because it was during the day there was no one there, you might see two or three people walking through, it was very quiet, but on weekends or whenever it was busy, it would have been busy; but for me, just on a normal week workday, that open area outside this grocery store was very quiet.

I went to the grocery store, I was trying so hard not to spend money and trying so hard to do this trip in my own strength. I'd been extremely disciplined with not spending and once again I was spending as little as I could.

I was standing in the queue at the checkout with my lunch waiting to pay for it. There was a large cripple black woman standing in front of me. She had wanted to buy something but at the till she had realized that she could not afford to pay for it. I felt compassion for her and then God prompted me strongly to buy it for her. I argued with Him about wasting money. The cashier put the item aside. The lady took the rest of her stuff, and she walked off. Next it was my turn to pay. I looked at her and figured that she was crippled, I could easily catch up to her. She walked away very slowly. I asked the Cashier to 'add it in,' and she added it into the bag with my lunch. Without looking at her item, after I paid, I headed off after her. I was walking behind her. She was in front of me, I could see her. She was about a metre in front of me. She turned the corner, entering the big open area in the mall. I pursued her. I turned the corner, and she was gone.

She had vanished into thin air. It was like she didn't exist! There was no one there. I was so unbelievably angry. I was angry that I had bought something for someone who was now gone. I was angry I'd spent money when I was already stripped of everything and had no way to buy my ticket to Hawaii. I was angry at God for prompting me to buy the item.

When I finished complaining and having my little tantrum, God said, "LOOK DOWN" and so I looked at what I was holding. "TURN IT OVER" He said. The item I had purchased was a tan fabric pencil case with a little plastic picture on the front. The picture was of a little RAINBOW over the word, "HAWAII."

Suddenly I was filled with trembling fear at the awe of God – because the rainbow was a sign from God to Noah after the flood, a sign of God's promise - I just knew in that moment, He was saying, that God was saying "I'm going to take you to Hawaii" and it was reassuring, "I promise you."

God told Noah it was a sign of His faithfulness to keep His promise that He would never flood the earth again. He keeps his promises. I said, "God I'm so sorry. I'm so sorry that I had such bad attitude and I'm so sorry that was angry at you. You know better, and I must not worry about money, you are going to sort this out."

I began to laugh. I realised she had disappeared because she was sent by God. She was an Angel, a supernatural messenger. I realised that God wanted to encourage me that I was not crazy for thinking of going to Hawaii; Hawaii was in His agenda. I was going to get there somehow, I just needed to trust Him on the details.

Money, money, money

So many money lessons. God's system is different to man's.

With the 'muffin money' that I had saved up, I went and bought a new suitcase for the trip. I was getting ready to go. My home was broken into, and the suitcase was stolen. They put almost all of my clothes, all my underwear, all my jewellery in it. They put everything that they could fit into the bag and took my bedding. They left me at very little stuff and off they went! I looked at the place where the suitcase had stood and thought, *"Am I insane?"*

In the end, I had no money left saved after re-buying some clothes, paying the required deposit for the course, buying the American Visa, and getting the required immunisations done. I had still not paid in full for my training course in advance and that bothered me. I borrowed a suitcase which I was obligated to return. *I was unable to fulfil that obligation in the end, which also bothered me.* I had an aeroplane ticket, but it was up to Los Angeles. I did not have an aeroplane ticket to fly from Los Angeles California, all the way across the ocean to Maui, Hawaii.

I left with SAR5.00, 5 South African Rand – (about 50c American) that would be useless the moment I left the ground.

The intensity of my prayers in my heart and mind increased. I was fearful yet I had supernatural peace. As I sat listening to the audio Bible (on cassette with a 'walkman') all the way on the flight, I was aware that I had an empty seat next to me. It felt like God himself was sitting there, like it was reserved for Him. I never felt alone for a second on the flights.

In the Bible it talks about your spirit and your flesh, and they are at war with each other all the time. My spirit was quite confident that God was going to do this, but my 'flesh' (soul: mind will and emotions) was so not sure. I thought I must be insane; who in their *right mind* is going to try and attempt what I'm doing, based on a pencil case with a rainbow picture and the word Hawaii? It was "foolishness" to man, but not to God.

The Bible says that we must walk by faith and by sight.[32] I had to learn about stepping out of this realm and stepping into the spiritual and living there. Living by faith.[33]

Memphis, Tennessee

The stopover in Memphis was lovely.

At one point I recall pleading with God for deliverance. He answered. When I left, an envelope was handed to me.

The Lord spoke clearly to my heart, as it was handed to me, saying: "50 IS FOR YOU." I did not know exactly how much money was in the envelope ($350), but I presumed what was in the envelope would cover the air ticket LA > Hawaii, and that $50 would be left over. I simply had to go.

I left and flew from Memphis to Los Angeles. I was heading off to Los Angeles believing that somehow, I'd get to Maui, Hawaii. Somehow the Lord would provide.

Conversion rate of the United States Dollar to the South African Rand was between 4-5 times. This means it was nearly 5 times harder for me to earn enough money. USD300 = ZAR1500 approximately.

Los Angeles airport: LAX

I arrived in LA airport on the 29th of June 1997, in my hands was $350 that I had received. The Lord had said, "$50 IS FOR YOU," and so I had presumed that the flight from LA to Maui, Hawaii would cost me $300 – but to my surprise when I went to buy the ticket it was $586!

I did not have enough money to purchase the ticket. I had enough money to change the date on the return ticket back to Johannesburg. Should I go home, accepting failure? I felt alone.

I never knew anybody around me in the California nor in the Los Angeles airport. I felt stuck on the other side of the world. Far away from home. Alone in a foreign airport with no significant amount of money.

I have been travelling for days and now I was exhausted. I just wanted to get to the destination, find the bed and fall asleep in it.

It was the last flight leaving for Hawaii, Maui and I could not get onto it.

I did not know what to do. I went to the bathroom and burst into tears. I got on to my knees and cried out to the Lord. I begged Him for miracle. I did not ask Him for money. I asked Him to get me to the other side – to get me to Maui.

I left the bathroom.

I decided that I would leave the bathroom and head towards the United Airlines boarding pass area. I recalled a story I'd heard of Corrie Ten Boon getting money for a ticket while she stood in the queue to buy it. I was believing that God would meet me, somehow, *along the way*. I expected a miracle. I did not know how but I expected a miracle.

I said to God "either you are real, or I am mad" as I left the bathroom.

God had to come through *if He was real*. I had to prove to myself that He was. I wanted to reassure myself that I was not crazy. And I wanted to prove it to my Dad and to show him that God was not "imaginary." I felt as if my sanity hung in the balance as I left the bathroom. Perhaps I was crazy? Perhaps my Dad was correct? Perhaps it was an "imaginary friend," and the existence of God was a lie. Perhaps God could not provide because He did not exist. My Dad had told me this my whole life that God did not exist, so perhaps my Dad was correct.

As I was walking towards the United Airlines boarding pass area, a middle-aged man that I had never seen before, came up to me. I thought perhaps he was taking pity on me. I probably looked terrible after crying in the bathroom. I do not recall the entire conversation. I do know that we spoke briefly and that I dismissed him as being "pushy." Later when I thought about it, I realised that this was *a very significant meeting.*

The man led me to a phone booth. I presume he paid for the call because I know that I didn't. He told me to phone my destination and tell them that I was coming. So, I did. Then he quickly took the phone from me (this was why I thought he was pushy). He told them that they had to quickly go and buy my ticket, that they must mention my age to get a discount on my ticket and they must pay for it. He said I would pay for it when I got to them.

I recall thinking, *"Oh no! what happens if I do not have enough money!"* and I was beckoning him to give me the phone – but before I could take the phone back to tell the people that I did not have enough money, he had put the phone down. He handed me his business card, told me to call if I needed anything else; and then almost commanded me, saying, "GOD IS WITH YOU; KEEP ON WALKING!"

At the time I did not realise how strange this meeting was. As I said, I dismissed him as being a pushy man. Instead of arguing with him, I continued to the United Airlines boarding pass area.

I arrived at the boarding pass area. I recognised the young

man behind the counter.

Journal entry 1998:

He was the young man who handed me a trolley when I didn't have a coin to loan a baggage trolley.

When I'd arrived that day, the young, blonde man had seen me struggling with my luggage. I didn't have a coin to get a baggage trolley. He handed me a baggage trolley to use. I was so grateful.

Here he was again. I sighed a sigh of relief as I stepped up to the counter. The familiar face was comforting.

I asked him, "Is there a ticket for me?" he looked at his screen and replied, "No." I smiled, and I went and sat down.

While I was sitting there a cleaner passed by. I was the last person left in the area. She asked what I was still doing there. I told her boldly, without hesitation that I was going to Maui, Hawaii. She said, "Oh, that plane is stalled on the runaway. They have a technical difficulty." She walked on.

I looked at my watch. As I looked down at my watch the Lord spoke to me very clearly saying, "GO BACK IN 20 MINUTES."

It was analogue and I counted 20 minutes. I didn't pay attention to the time because I figured it was probably in the wrong time zone. After 20 minutes I stood up and returned to the young man. I asked again if someone had bought me a ticket. He explained that he had logged off his computer, but that he would log back on and check.

"YES! Here it is." He said and printed my boarding pass.

I was escorted to the plane. The plane, which was already on the runway waiting to leave. But it hadn't taken off. Within a short time, I was on the aircraft. The technical fault had been resolved, the minute I closed my seat belt, it was announced that we were leaving. Everybody on the aeroplane was cheering, including me – I was cheering God for His miracle. I was on the last plane going to Maui and I was beyond happy! There was a 50th airline celebration. On the aeroplane the cabin crew were in a party mood. It was a very happy flight!

"So do not fear, for I am with you; do not be dismayed, for I am your God. I will strengthen you and help you; I will uphold you with My righteous right hand"

Isaiah 41:10

"He gives strength to the weary and increases the power of the weak" Isaiah 40:29

Angels in LAX airport

The young blonde man helping me was interesting. I was left with a sense of peace. I did have a "tingle" or "funny feeling," my face may even have gone red, but I was focused on what I was doing and never gave it too much thought at the time. They say, angels appear as young men.

I also find *the cleaner* an interesting person. Maybe she knew about what was happening on the runway because maybe they had communication between the cleaners on the ground inside the airport and those on the runaway. I presume that different parts of the airport have different cleaners with different assignments, especially for a large airport like LAX. I don't think she had any communication with the aeroplane. *To me it was as if, when she spoke it, the plane got stalled.*

My understanding of the spiritual realm is that it was as I declared by faith, *(believing what I couldn't yet see)*[20] that I was going to Hawaii *(knowing that there were no more flights to Hawaii, Maui that day)* – that she declared, *(a prophetic assignment),* what she had been on the scene to do. (*Angels are God's messengers and they carry out His assignments. She'd been assigned this task when I prayed in LA in the toilet).* When she declared *the plane was stalled*, I think that maybe the plane *got stalled* with a technical difficulty.

The "technicality" was that I was supposed to be on it!

Journal entry June 1997:

I was sitting on United Airline Flight NW0551 on 29 June 1997 in Los Angeles. The engines were running, the aeroplane was moving on the runway. It was heading towards the take-off position. I felt the engines roar, the plane edging forwards. Faster and faster, it went – and then the plane tilted, the wheels lifted. We were off the ground! – that sinking feeling in my tummy as we soared up in the air and I began to cry.

The exploding joy inside me was something I could not explain in words. It was Glorious! Just moments before I had no ticket, ha! in fact I still had no ticket! God had made a way where there seemed to be no way.

"But those who hope in the LORD will renew their strength. They will soar on wings like eagles; they will run and not grow weary; they will walk and not be faint."

Isaiah 40:31

Maui, Hawaii June 97 to September 97

When I reached my destination, members of the organisation that I had called, were waiting at the airport to greet me. They had bought my ticket. I was surprised that they recognised me. They had never seen me before. Maybe I was just out of place looking. They told me that they had purchased my ticket and it had cost them $300. I handed over the $300! Which left "$50 for me." I did not tell them, but I remember the huge sense of gratitude when they said it was only $300. I recall thinking in my heart, *"Thank you Jesus,"* and smiling in that moment.

Before I arrived in Memphis, my bag (hand luggage deemed too big) had gotten lost, leaving the gifts behind for my friends; it also had my toiletries. For the stopover I had used the aeroplane toothbrush supplied on the plane which had enough toothpaste for the extra night. This meant that when I reached Hawaii, I did not have my own toiletries (a proper toothbrush, and cleaning products like shower gel, shampoo, and conditioner). I did have toothpaste in my main suitcase which held my clothes. I still had some tubes of Colgate toothpaste!

Journal USA 1997:

(A young girl) made me laugh out loud! When she saw all the toothpaste she said, "Didn't you think we would have toothpaste in the USA?"

The organisation was YWAM, Maui. (YWAM stands for YOUTH WITH A MISSION). In due course I would discover team members said it stood for YOUTH WITHOUT ANY MONEY. They understood how God provides.

I was taken to the girls' dormitory. It was like a large house with a kitchen and a bathroom, and each room had bunk beds in it. I was taken to a small room with two beds.

Everybody had a "welcome pack" on their bed. It was a lei of flowers (Hawaiian Frangipani's strung together in a necklace) with sweets in the middle.

Mine was a lei of flowers with toiletries in the middle. The team of people at the base had been praying for each of us before our arrival and had felt that God had directed them to give me a new toothbrush, shampoo, and other toiletries. He provided my every need.

God even provided me with some more appropriate sandals for the beach. I had arrived onto this tropical island with my nose ring, black clothes, and black Doc Martins (ankle length lace-up boots).

The first thing I did with the $50 was bought a phone calling card from the base's office so that I could phone home from the call box and let my Mom know that I had arrived safely in Hawaii. The next call that I made was to the number on the business card from the "pushy" man at the airport. I had assumed him to be a pushy man, but he had helped me, and I wanted to thank him.

When I called the number, the Operator said, "THIS NUMBER DOES NOT EXIST." I tried again. The number still, did not exist.

The card is still in my possession. A reminder to me of the fear that I felt because I chewed the one corner of it while I waited those twenty minutes. It is also a reminder that God makes a way where there seems to be no way. That the Lord is faithful. He answers prayers. He sends Angels.

The experience with the business card reminded me of something that happened six years before.

I needed to get my driver's license. Mom had dropped me off and said, "You better get it today," and she headed off to work. My new boss had said the job was dependent on me getting my driver's license.

Journal recalling 1991:

As I sat alone in the driving testing station, an older lady sat down on the bench next to me. We spoke and I told her that if I didn't get my license that day, I would be losing my job she handed me her business card and said I wasn't to worry about my job, if I lost my job I could come and work for her. She was an interior designer/decorator. The card gave me peace of mind I thought that would be a lovely job, to work for an interior designer. It doesn't matter if I lose my job, I'll be OK. The card gave me peace of mind.

What happened when I returned to work:

After I had passed my license and received it that day. I phoned the number on the card to say, 'thank you for the offer but I'd still be able to continue with my job' - but when I called the number, the number did not exist. I was irritated and threw the card in the rubbish bin.

Instead of seeing it as an Angelic intervention. It wasn't until this Hawaii experience that I realised that *this* old lady was *also* one of God's messenger angels. I recalled the peace that had flooded me as I did my driver's test.

Your husband is not here

One day while I was in Hawaii, I was invited to hear a guest speaker. I was told that he was South African, like me. I went not knowing that I had been invited to hear a "prophet." I would probably not have gone if someone told me he was a "Prophet" because I had very briefly been exposed to the sections of Christianity that had people called "Prophets" and I thought that these churches were like cults. He was a different kind of 'Prophet' to that kind.

This man very accurately told me, "YOUR HUSBAND IS NOT HERE, I don't know why I am telling you this."

I knew. God knew. It is so funny how God can pick on you in a meeting and not embarrass you publicly because no one knows what the Lord is saying and yet it is something so huge and profound to you. *(It was the first time that it happened to me but not the last time).*

I had hoped in my heart that perhaps God was sending me to Hawaii to meet my husband. I was 24 turning 25 and beginning to wonder if I'd be left "an old maid" because all my peers were getting married, and I was beginning to feel like I was being left on the shelf. Quietly in my mind I had been analysing every single man I met. I was wasting a lot of brain energy! God was basically a loving father disciplining his child saying, "STOP IT!" He put a stop to it, BOOM! HE IS NOT HERE!

God had in fact sent my husband-to-be from his coastal life inland to Johannesburg, South Africa. While I was "globe-trotting" or "circling the flat earth" (?) he was studying.

This man also told me other things. In those days he used to record his words and give you a cassette tape with what he had said. Everything that he had said came true. And then I threw away the cassette as I felt it had served its purpose. The things he said took several years to happen, without any manipulation from me.

From Hawaii I was invited to California by a lovely family who paid for my ticket to fly from Hawaii back to LA. They arranged accommodation for the next almost two months! And spoilt me for my 25th birthday.

I returned to South Africa briefly after the USA and began sharing my stories with others. My travels and stories inspired others to take a leap of faith (and you can do it too.) I left again and went to Europe, then on to the Middle East.

16. A LEAP OF FAITH

Art supplier who became a Horse Dentist

Wayne's Testimony

"But without faith it is impossible to please Him."

Hebrews 11:6

That is certainly true in my life.

I was practically born on a horse. My life is still intertwined with this industry today. I started my career in competitive show jumping at the age of 9.

Keeping horses can be costly, and my Mom made sure I found a way to pay for part of their keep.

At age twenty I was employed by a family friend and well-known Art Supplier in Johannesburg. I worked for them for fifteen long years. Long enough to supply Nathalie with some art materials and receive a push in the FAITH direction.

I liked the familiarity of life. It was safe and comfortable but going nowhere slowly. Embarking on a different career path crossed my mind, but I was reluctant to do so, as I had a wife and kids to support. Or so I thought!

I received an unexpected call from another showjumper, who introduced me to this "new profession" in South Africa, called horse dentistry. He encouraged me to check it out. After some research we found that courses were only available overseas.

With a small salary and a mound of debt, enrolling for this course was not an option. I chewed on this idea for two years, but never took the step to do anything about it.

Nathalie and my wife happened to have one of their coffee dates when I arrived home from work. They listened to me complain about working for a boss, and I mentioned how I wished I could go to America to do the equine dentistry course.

I'll never forget Nathalie's words to me: *"So? Why don't you? Just do it!"*

Those words propelled me into lending the money and doing the course in the United States. Everything just fell into place.

Upon completion of the course the plan was to do

dentistry part time. God had other plans, and within three months I earned more through dentistry than in my full-time job.

We've never looked back since. We know where this business comes from. It is only God's mercy, provision, and His hand that worked everything to our good!

Wayne Dale

Dale Equine Dental Care cc.

Nathalie: WORD OF ENCOURAGEMENT

Wayne looked despondent as he walked in. I offered a word of encouragement to take a leap of faith. My life had been my testament. He was brave enough to act on that word. I believe he operated under the Holy Spirit's "GIFT OF FAITH." Faith that is a special kind of faith for a special task, not 'salvation faith'.

17. THE CENTRE OF THE WORLD

I was questioning everything I'd been told about "The Christ" and Jesus. I went on a search for "Truth" about who Jesus was and found many "truths."

After I left school and was working, I studied a university short course; an overview on The 5 Major Religions of the World: Judaism, Christianity, Hinduism, Buddhism, and Islam (the Muslim faith). My search led me to eventually reading The Qur'an and the Book of Mormon, in parts. My discovery was that all the major religions of the world recognised Jesus: as a prophet, a good man, an enlightened person, a false Messiah, or a God. Not all religions recognised: Buddha, Joseph Smith, or Muhammed. My conclusion was: *there is something different about Jesus.* He stood out like a main character in a play. Even the date we write down every day was based around Him. But WHO IS JESUS? It seemed like many people were saying who Jesus was, but they were not all saying the same thing.

I had the wonderful privilege of visiting Israel in 1998 directly after I left the Netherlands, where I had been living in the Red-Light district of Amsterdam.

Israel was the land where Jesus had walked as a young child and later as a miracle worker with his twelve disciples.

Condensed summary: I stayed there for about three months. Travelling first directly to Tel Aviv from Schiphol airport, then to Jerusalem where I spent my first week. From there I travelled north, eventually staying in Metula, in the farthest northern part of the country. Seeing many places in Northern Israel on the way. Then I travelled south all the way to Eilat, in the farthest southern part, stopping at Tzaft (Safed), Haifa and some other places, before Jerusalem down to Eilat. From Eilat, crossing the desert, going to Egypt. A few weeks later returning to Dahab, then back up to Eilat, Israel. Traveling back north to Beersheva and then back to Jerusalem again, before returning to Tel Aviv airport and heading out to Germany.

Jerusalem has a section called "The Old City." It was one of my favourite places! The rest of 'Jerusalem' is a busy modern city. The Old City has stone alley ways filled with little hawkers selling their wares. Bustling with people, fragrances, and colours. Ladies sat on the floor making flat breads. I'd grown to love eating the flat bread with a type of Greek style yoghurt that I'd been introduced to in Acre.

Jerusalem is the centre of world religions. It is a significant place to all three mono-theist World religions: Jewish, Islamic and Christian.

Armenian quarter

I discovered that Jerusalem's old city was divided into "quarters": The Jewish quarter, the Muslim quarter, the Christian quarter, and the Armenian quarter. It seemed to me that the Armenian quarter was very 'unknown' and kept to themselves. I feel that Armenia needs to have its' say here, in a sense, as I spoke about the Jewish and Muslim quarters in my pervious story.

It wasn't until I did the *JeffMara Podcast* that I met a kind Armenian person who took the time to explain some things to me. I discovered that Armenia is very significant to Christianity. The females hold a powerful position in their culture. The first Queen of Jerusalem was Armenian.

Mothers are the centre of the family. They do not celebrate Christmas on the 25th December with the rest of the world but celebrate Christmas and New Years on the same day since the birth of Christ marks day 1. Armenia is believed to be the place of the Garden of Eden, as well as having Mt Ararat, where Noah's Ark landed; so, it is the place of the beginnings of human biblical history. They are Christian too; in fact, they were the first official Christian kingdom. Jesus' disciples Bartholomew and Thaddeus were the disciples who took the Gospel to Armenia.

This recent discovery for me about Armenia has led me to wanting to read more, but unfortunately books were burned throughout history. It seems mostly Paul's letters (epistles) are recorded in the Bible and not all the other disciples who were with Jesus. I'd love to speak to Bartholomew and Thaddeus if it were possible or find out if they wrote anything down for us.

I have much to learn. I'm sure that there is a library of earth's history in heaven. I will be spending some time in there one day. If you are looking for me, try the library!

18. WOULD THE REAL GOD PLEASE STAND UP

The 'world' wants me to believe that we have a Supreme Being, ONE God above all. They want me to believe that it doesn't matter if you want to call 'it' Allah, Hashem, Jehovah, YHVH, G-D, Creator, Father, or SELF (or making self the I AM). Any road leads to the same God (because the One God is ultimately myself in some cases). You can call him anything but just not Jesus!

It didn't feel like "one God over all" when I was there, in the centre of world religions. It felt like one place, three religions were fighting over. Three religions who each claimed *their* God was the only true God. (Allah, YHVH or the Triune God: Father Son Holy Spirit.) I felt disappointed in organised religions. They all failed to **love** people outside of their religion.

Who is God? For me the story about Elijah and the Prophets of Baal really brings to light who God is. It is clear in this that not all roads lead to the One God.

I **do** believe there is only One God. I do **not** believe that He is 'myself'. I AM connected to I AM, but He is the GREAT I

AM.

Summary: Elijah duels with the prophets of Baal on Mt. Carmel, north-western Israel. After Baal is shown to be an inefficacious deity, Elijah's God, the One true God, shows up in a splendour and dramatically consumes Elijah's sacrifice in front of all the people. The people kill the prophets of Baal, King Ahab flees.

I love this story so much from the long version, that I have decided to share it here. It just says it so much better than I do:

God or Baal on Mount Carmel [35]

from 1 Kings 18 (NASB)

[20] So Ahab sent orders among all the sons of Israel and brought the prophets together at Mount Carmel. [21] Then Elijah approached all the people and said, "How long are you going to [a]struggle with the two choices? If the LORD is God, follow Him; but if Baal, follow him." But the people did not answer him so much as a word. [22] Then Elijah said to the people, "I alone am left as a prophet of the LORD, while Baal's prophets are 450 men. [23] Now have them give us two oxen; and have them choose the one ox for themselves and cut it up, and place it on the wood, but put no fire under it; and I will prepare the other ox and lay it on the wood, and I will not put a fire under it. [24] Then you call on the name of your god, and I will call on the name of the LORD; and the God who answers by fire, He is God." And all

the people replied, "[h]That is a good idea."

²⁵ So Elijah said to the prophets of Baal, "Choose the one ox for yourselves and prepare it first, since there are many of you, and call on the name of your god, but put no fire under the ox." ²⁶ Then they took the ox which was given them and they prepared it, and they called on the name of Baal from morning until noon, saying, "O Baal, answer us!" But there was no voice, and no one answered. And they limped about the altar which they had made. ²⁷ And at noon Elijah ridiculed them and said, "Call out with a loud voice, since he is a god; undoubtedly, he is attending to business, or is on the way, or is on a journey. Perhaps he is asleep and will awaken." ²⁸ So they cried out with a loud voice and cut themselves according to their custom with swords and lances until blood gushed out on them. ²⁹ When midday was past, they raved until the time of the offering of the evening sacrifice; but there was no voice, no one answered, and no one paid attention. ³⁰ Then Elijah said to all the people, "Come forward to me." So, all the people came forward to him. And he repaired the altar of the LORD which had been torn down. ³¹ Then Elijah took twelve stones, corresponding to the number of the tribes of the sons of Jacob, to whom the word of the LORD had come, saying, "Israel shall be your name." ³² And with the stones he built an altar in the name of the LORD; and he made a trench around the altar, large enough to hold two measures of seed. ³³ Then he laid out the wood, and he cut the ox in pieces and placed it on the wood. ³⁴ And he said, "Fill four large jars with water and pour it on the burnt offering and on the wood." And he said, "Do it a second time," so they did it a second time. Then he said, "Do it a third time," so they did it a third time. ³⁵ The water flowed around the altar, and he also filled the trench with water.

Elijah's Prayer

36 Then at the time of the offering of the evening sacrifice, Elijah the prophet approached and said, "Lord, God of Abraham, Isaac, and Israel, today let it be known that You are God in Israel and that I am Your servant, and that I have done all these things at Your word. **37** Answer me, Lord, answer me, so that this people may know that You, Lord, are God, and that You have turned their heart back." **38** Then the fire of the Lord fell and consumed the burnt offering and the wood, and the stones and the dust; and it licked up the water that was in the trench. **39** When all the people saw this, they fell on their faces; and they said, "The Lord, He is God; the Lord, He is God!" **40** Then Elijah said to them, "Seize the prophets of Baal; do not let one of them escape." So, they seized them; and Elijah brought them down to the brook Kishon and slaughtered them there.

41 Now Elijah said to Ahab, "Go up, eat and drink; for there is the sound of the roar of a heavy shower." **42** So Ahab went up to eat and drink. But Elijah went up to the top of Carmel; and he bent down to the earth and put his face between his knees. **43** And he said to his servant, "Go up now, look toward the sea." So, he went up and looked, but he said, "There is nothing." Yet Elijah said, "Go back" seven times. **44** And when he returned the seventh time, he said, "Behold, a cloud as small as a person's hand is coming up from the sea." And Elijah said, "Go up, say to Ahab, 'Harness your chariot horses and go down, so that the heavy shower does not stop you.'" **45** Meanwhile the sky became dark with clouds and wind came up, and there was a heavy shower. And Ahab rode and went to Jezreel. **46** Then the hand of the Lord was on Elijah, and he belted his cloak around *his waist and outran Ahab to Jezreel.*

When I got to see the Holy Land, I was given the opportunity by a lady to see this site – she took me to Mt. Carmel, Israel.

I would encourage Christians go and see Israel and the old city of Jerusalem for themselves if it is at all possible. The experience was life-changing. The Holy Bible in the flesh! Marvellous!

However, I wasn't another starry-eyed tourist believing all the nonsense fed to me by a tour guide, so maybe that made the big difference on my perspectives.

I was living there, helping the locals, and seeing how they were being treated by the "Christian" tourists and how the "Christians" were treating the sites. The Christians were not very loving nor kind to the locals.

Some tourist guides would say things that were blatantly wrong but if people haven't read or studied the Bible, they would just lap it all up as if it is the truth. They are just trying to make a living. They don't care if they get the sites wrong.

One guide sold 'Holy water' that we refilled from the tap, and I said to him, "but this isn't 'Holy water' it hasn't been 'blessed'" – he remarked, "everything from the Holy land is Holy, we sell the Holy sand too and they buy it…"

In my opinion Christians who haven't read their Bible, should stop listening to podcasts, preachers and reading other books and make reading THE HOLY BIBLE once through *at least* as a desperately important goal and priority. Read it, for yourself and then listen to the preachers and see if they are even preaching what it says.

All Bibles have been changed. Do not let that deter you from reading it. There are Bibles that have been changed into interpretations instead of translations from the original. That is another way that the message has been changed. I'm not a "1611 KJV only" advocate. I recommend you learn to read the original version, but seen as I haven't managed that myself, I guess we must settle for an English transliteration or translation, not an interpretation. Side note: "The Passion translation" is not a "translation" it is a paraphrase like The Message Bible. These are delightful to read, nevertheless. For an English translation, look for CJB, NASB, KJV, NKJV. Things have been changed over time, but just read it – once through.

The outside shell may be marred but the spiritual has been kept well hidden. A dirty penny is just as valuable as a clean penny.

19. RELIGION IS MESSY

I came away from a few years of Bible college and doing Christian missionary work, into a Christian marriage several years later, never having heard of all the "traditional Christian things." I did not do any of them. On the "mission field" and I'd landed up at home for every Christmas through all those years. I'd never spent a Christmas away from my family. I'd never had a "traditional Christian Christmas." I did not know what "the advent" was, nor "ash Wednesday" or any other traditions and rituals that Christians do. If it's not recorded in the Bible as things to do, I only knew what was in there. I was literally "living under a Rock."

> *"I love you Lord, my strength. The LORD is my rock, my fortress, and my deliverer; my God is my rock in whom I take refuge, my shield and the horn of my salvation, my stronghold. Psalms 18:1-2*

A 'good Christian church missionary' would point you to their 'good Christian church'. I failed to be a good Christian missionary, as they failed me, to be a good Christian church. There is no good Christian church(es), sorry, if you are looking for a "perfect Christian church" you will not find it– because *you* are there! They ALL have imperfect people in them, and you and I are imperfect people too. "Christian idealism" is so stifling and rigid.

In Israel I saw a new perspective on Christianity and the "gullible sheep" followers. It was eye-opening. I disliked all things "religious." Jesus didn't like the 'religious' stuff either.

From my perspective, it was very upsetting to see all the Catholic Christian churches on all the "sites," *claiming* them. It felt a bit selfish to me, like "He's *our God* and you cannot have him unless you join our church" ...meanwhile

JESUS IS FOR EVERYONE.

It was an overarching feeling I got in Jerusalem, it wasn't just "a Catholic thing." It was a selfish, self-righteous, "religious" thing.

I am not anti-Catholic.

Maree's testimony.

I first met Nathalie on the school bench waiting for my youngest to finish class. We got talking and I felt an instant connection. It is interesting how the Lord can bring people together from totally different backgrounds and denominations. The Catholic and a Protestant make an interesting friend combination. For almost 20 years I have greatly appreciated Nathalie's love for the Lord Jesus, her Bible teaching, and artistic gifts, enclosed in a passion for people from all walks of life. Our friendship has been a true blessing.

She painted a Biblical themed wall mural for us in the entrance of our home. The mural has an effect on everyone who enters our house. We all love it, but some hate it. The builder walked in and told me straight away that he did not want to discuss religion, but his offsider said that it was such a privilege to meet a Christian family, that the mural really spoke to him, particularly being just after Easter. He said that he had worked in the area for over 20 years, and he had never walked into a house with anything like it. Our young tiler felt quite at home and was questioning why he no longer believed in God. All up, it is really interesting to see how different people react to the artwork. The door opens for some interesting conversations.

Nathalie – **A TRUE FRIEND IS HARD TO FIND** I was lonely. We had moved countries. October 2005, I sat outside the school looking across at the mothers and noticed these very interesting jeans. They were bold, creative, and eccentric. I became friends with her because of her pants! Little did I know that the "bold" lady wearing them was the quietest, most gentle soul I had ever met in my life. She has been the closest person to me, no matter where I have lived. Walked with me through the worst days of my life, loved me through my dirtiest house stages and my most unlovely times of mommy-ing four little children. She was always patient and kind. Remembering all my children's birthdays and sending gifts for them every year for Christmas. I've always felt she was like a sister to me, my children have always felt like she was like an aunt. She just adopted me and loved me. I loved her back the only way I knew how. I painted her a wall mural.

20. THE DARK SIDE

Well, here is a whole chapter I did not intend on writing. Let's talk about the darkness. The angels (fallen ones, aka demons and other spirits), that are not pleasant to deal with. I'll group them together under the banner of "demons/demonic" for this chapter.

Jesus cast out demons. Demons and all kinds of spirits must submit to the Lord, even if they don't want to, they have to. It is the order of things. They know who He is.

"The Universe," if you want to call it that, responds to us (the good side and the bad side). We are all connected. Our actions have ripple effects. Cause and effect.

Consequences for actions. We can choose to persist on our own little path of struggle, to do things our way. We have a free will. But the choices we make will have ripple effects. They will have consequences. Sometimes we persist on a path that leads us into being ensnared. The path of destruction. Some people wrestle their 'demons,' other people are completely taken over by demonic entities.

Street march

An early encounter with a demon was on a street march through Johannesburg declaring "Jesus is Lord" and singing songs to praise Him. A lady approached me. A demonic entity had taken over a lady's body. I spoke to the lady, but a male voice replied, *"You don't know who I am, do you?"* Recognising the voice was a demonic voice, I said, "bow down in the name of Jesus" to this entity – to which the lady bowed, and then I naively said, "GO" – because I recalled Jesus telling the demons to GO - to which the lady run as fast as she could away from me. I had so much regret over telling the devil to go. I knew that there must have been a better way. A way that would have helped *the woman* to be free of the demonic spirit. I knew that I still had much to learn.

Devil's advocate

Another encounter happened on a mission's trip into Zambia. I saw this entity manifesting in the lady's face, much like the movie, "The Devil's Advocate," where the movie shows the demonic entity crawling under the skin inside the person's body. It seemed that another lady saw it too. No one else seemed to see it but in that moment we both knew that we both saw it.

The dark shadow man or presence

One day I was standing in a venue that I had leased for a new Art studio. I had unpacked all my stuff into the venue with my family and my husband headed home. I told him I would lock up and follow shortly but I wanted to pray first.

As I stood there praying over the venue, a presence came into the room and I said, "Oh hello"

I obviously became aware of it and surprised myself with my little chirpy greeting. I then said, "I hope we can work together." *Honestly, what was I thinking? Darkness and light don't work together!*

In my prayers I had been claiming the place for Jesus and obviously this "being" oversaw this place or had the title-deed. I was just a tenant and it decided to evict me.

That night the place was broken into and the next morning when I went to the Art Studio, all my things were stolen, except one painting: a prophetic painting about the Holy Spirit's "new oil."

With no art materials and the studio cleaned out, teaching art abruptly came to a halt, forcing me to use what I had - my husband's computer to type up and publish *'Discovering an Artist'*. Then slowly rebuild my art supplies, one tube of paint at a time.

In summary – they do exist. It is not some person pretending or mentally unstable or putting on a show. These beings do exist, and they do take up habitation in some people.

Believers Authority

Deliverance. I believe that sometimes it is necessary to cast out demons. To tell them to GO. We must use the authority we have as the Kings children, under the Blood of the Lamb and His Name.

It is not our place to shout at the devil, call him insulting names, even the archangel would not dare to do that! Jude v 9-10.

I will not be teaching further on this topic in this book, merely stating that it is another area.

HEIDI- **DELIVERED FROM DEPRESSION**

Heidi's testimony

Six years ago, Nathalie prayed with me about Depression. I had been on anti-depressants for years. I was used to living with it. It was part of my life. I had prayed many times before that. It didn't work. I was even suicidal.

When we prayed the Lord took the depression away. Instantly.

A little while later I got some anti-depressants because I was feeling down. They made me so sick. A doctor told me to throw them away. I threw them in the bin, and I've never had any anti-depressants again.

God has filled me with joy. I believe God has really used Nathalie in my life.

Nathalie – **DELIVERANCE** and PATIENCE, IN LOVE

God told me to walk alongside Heidi and listen to His guidance. We met 10 years ago. First, we walked through the process of encouraging her in the things of Lord and inviting her to a ladies Bible Study at my house. Then a little while later through the Baptism of the Holy Spirit. After that, God began a deeper healing work in her life, deliverance from demonic influences. One of the first things to go was the Spirit of depression. In its place God filled her with His joy. Her life now is a testimony of God's goodness. She has touched many people around her.

Some people 'demonise' everything that they don't understand. If you saw an angel, they tell you it was a demon. Abraham was visited by angels. Mary was visited by the angel Gabriel, "angelic visitation" not a demon. When the message is important enough, they appear. In fact, there is no light in the demonic. It cannot appear as light, and that verse is misrepresented about the fallen angels appearing as angels of light, they have no light.

They are cunning, can trick, lie, and deceive.

Many things are demonised and misrepresented. Not all things that are demonised are demonic:

Crystals. I don't have any, (because I am a minimalist, who likes SPACE, and I don't like having clutter around) but I love God's creations. I love stones and rocks. Texture and nature. Crystals and precious gemstones come in so many colours. They are in the Bible. Such beauty when you don't demonise it. Why do we demonise this beauty? The High priest wore a breastplate with different precious stones to represent different tribes. I think the very minerals on earth hold special significance to God.

Incense and burning candles, and fire. The priests lit the incense in the temple, and they lit the menorah: 7 branch candle stick, that represents the Holy Spirit or "the 7 Spirits of God" of Isaiah 11:1-3. Why do we demonise incense, candles, and fire?

Just because the devil uses what God has created, doesn't mean that what God created is demonic. Everything that God created was beautiful and good.

It is my hope that when people discover me, they discover Him. That readers don't feel like they must join some church, perform some ritual, or do something demonic to find Him, to receive their healing, to have a blessed life. He really wants to bless people abundantly, who love Him.

PART 5: THE LIGHT

Title: Crossing Over   Oil painting by Nathalie de Wet

The painting that I used for the cover of "Adventures in the Light"

21. THE NEAR-DEATH EXPERIENCE

It was important to me to explain to the reader the mentality toward the crime in South Africa in the 1990's, how we normalised it and how language was downplayed. I went into detail to explain this in my previous book, so I won't repeat all that here. I went into detail about what lead me to this point in my life. Details of the home invasion that I'm not going to rehash all of that again in this book. If you would like to know more about the surrounding details, please read my other book. Let's keep this one LIGHT.

The crimes being committed were so bad, that it was mild in comparison. Most importantly, people who did not have a "mild assault" came away from it dead. I was not dead, so it was "mild."

The police did not take any fingerprints. I was told I was alive, I was only stabbed with a small blade, which had not taken off any of my body parts – so I was OK. I was also told that the attack was *my fault* for not having my door locked and that I needed to *get over it* and learn from this to lock my door. I was even ridiculed and reminded of the nursery rhyme about the three little pigs who didn't let the wolf in. Told, if my door was locked, they would not have come in.

South Africans had an "adapt or die" mentality. You get used to adapting. Life goes on, you get over it. For me the attack was simply a bump in the road. I pretty much forgot about it and moved on with my life. It wasn't the reason I left South Africa. It was just a pothole in the road, just another theft. A more violent one, but just another one.

I didn't think my experience would be of any significance to others. I'm sad that I took so long to realise that by sharing my story, I could help others.

Over recent years I have begun helping people to understand their pain, their children's suicides, or family deaths. I began to realise that telling my story could help other people.

The trauma was so intense (not mild at all), that it forced my soul-spirit to jump out of my body. This is called an "out of body experience," because mine was associated with, "life-threatening," being shot and stabbed multiple times, it was considered a "near-death experience."

The day of the event

On the 18th of February 1999 I invited my friend over for coffee after work. It was a beautiful hot Summer's day in February. Late afternoon after work, early evening. The grass outside was lush and green. The garden surrounding the cottage I'd just recently moved into had heaps of potential. I was looking forward to weeding on the weekends and fixing up the overgrown flowerbeds. I had a large garden spade sitting inside the house next to the bathroom wall, just waiting for me to dig around those flower beds and tidy them up.

He arrived just after work, that must've been around five o'clock in the evening. I made him tea on myself coffee. In the Middle East I'd been sitting on the floor quite a lot, in his house I used to sit on the floor, when he came to visit me, we sat on the floor.

We were sitting with the glass double door open letting in the summer breeze. (The police later accused me of being the one at fault, for having my door open. I should have known better).

Relaxed and happy, I had handed him his mug and sat down. I placed my mug on the floor next to me. I hadn't sipped it yet.

A young, black man walked straight in through the open door. I looked at him standing next to me. He greeted me with a smile on his face and a slight bow of his head, as it is done in Africa. A bow of the head is a greeting, 'hello.' I smiled back. It never occurred to me that walking in without knocking was impolite because it was something that African people do in Africa. A knock was not required.

My friend thought that he must be the gardener. This is what he told me later because the man seemed quite friendly. I asked in a friendly inquiring tone, *"Can I help you?"* I had no idea who he was. I'd never seen him before.

He walked up to me, and put his index finger to his lips, and he said, "sssh" (the way a teacher would do when they tell the class to be quiet).

I was thinking, "W*hy?*" but before I could utter a word, he put his gun on my forehead. The cold 9mm Parabellum gun was pressed hard onto my forehead. He had no concern with how hard he was pressing it into my skin. My eyes caught sight of the next man entering in, and I could see that there were others behind him. This was a gang.

As he had put the gun to my head, my friend who was military trained, jumped forward to grab the gun but the others came in, surrounded my friend, and restrained him. He was told to sit down.

The man holding the gun to my head caught my attention. With the gun to my head, he looked straight at me into my eyes and told me in a quiet voice to be calm. Then he said it would be OK - and he squeezed the trigger.

I let out an uncontrollable hysterical screen. I was shaking, uncontrollably, like a leaf. He had pulled the trigger.

(My physical body was probably still screaming, but where I was, I wasn't screaming).

I was in the light.

It's as if time stood still. Yet time carried on at normal pace. In this realm, on the earth realm, what happened was in a split second, I don't know, less than a split second, but where I was, I continued in normal time. Time didn't speed up nor slow down, it just continued.

(for me it was as if I went on a half an hour journey.)

Let's go on that journey together now:

My soul-spirit – left the physical body. I travelled faster than lightning speed towards The Light. I was instantly in the light. There was no tunnel or light at the end of the tunnel.

I was completely in The Light and I knew The Light; it was Jesus. The Light of the world.

When you look at the light it's like that *Shekinah* glory that He is surrounded by. An incredibly bright, pure, white light. This ball of LIFE, energy, and love. This figure coming out of the light, and yet He is the light.

I was on my knees. I wasn't looking at him. Bowing down saying, "Lord, have mercy." My first reaction was, "Lord, have mercy" because I knew that I had just been so rebellious, and I had made this choice to be so disgusting. In the presence of God, we judge ourselves. Adam and Eve did it in the garden of Eden. They hid from God. They judged themselves and their own actions. They knew that they had done wrong. It is called "the conviction of the Holy Spirit" It doesn't condemn us, but it convicts us.

He was talking to me and so we had a conversation.

Because of all the spiritual things that had happened, happened before the assault, during my life, I had these promises: about my husband, and about children. He had said that MY HUSBAND'S NAME WOULD START WITH AN R. *(I used to call him "Mr. Right" in my journals)* God had told me my daughter's name, and He told me the date I was going to get married, *(but not the year)* and he gave me the date and he said, "IT'S A SET DATE" *(It came to pass on that date).*

In our conversation I was talking to Him, and I was saying, "But what about all these things? What about the husband? What about the daughter that you told me about? What about the date?"

It felt like half an hour. I'm just in normal time just carrying on with time.

I didn't have what others call, "a life review," nor seen any screens with my life being played to me or anything, He just said that I could come home.

He said that I could go back into my body. Well, He didn't say, "go back into your body" He said, "IT'S OK IF YOU WANT TO DIE NOW OR YOU CAN CHOOSE TO LIVE" and I thought, "I want to live"

He said, "OK, BUT IT WILL BE A STRUGGLE"

I was instantly back inside my body.

Back inside my body

It ended like this:

I returned into my body. I was now fully back in my body and back in earthly time.

At this point the gun had it's trigger pulled. The man pulled the gun away slightly from my head. He looked confused. The bullet had travelled down the barrel of the gun to my forehead and when the guy moved the gun away. The bullet fell and dropped into my lap and then it rolled down onto the floor.

That entire spiritual experience, that felt like a conversation was so quick, less than a split second. The time in the two 'realms' is so different.

The man was angry, so he took the gun and whacked me on the side of the head, but I was fine I didn't lose consciousness or anything. (I just realised it was a real gun and not a plastic pretend one, that what was happening was very serious.)

In my other book, I explained what was happening in the physical or 'natural' realm. The ordeal went on for many hours.

It was a struggle. My hands were tied up behind my back with a wire coat hanger. The men were hurting me, trying to rape me, and stabbing me repeatedly, with a knife.

Guardian angel

Very suddenly, I felt two hands on mine untwisting the wire coat hanger. Somebody was untwisting the wire. I could physically feel the wire was being untwisted and pressing against my skin and the wire getting looser. Somebody's hands were doing this, and it was not one of the four men. There is no logical explanation as to what happened with my hands. The young man who had been standing guard over me at one point earlier, was no longer there, he had run off to loot the house. Nobody was standing behind me now.

The wire was loose enough for me to pull out my left hand. I was able to grab the fingers that were digging into my neck, and I pulled the hand off my neck. With my right hand, as soon as it broke free from the wire, I pulled the stuff out of my mouth and gasped for more air. (The way they gagged me was disgusting, the thought of it still makes me tremble.)

With my mouth available to scream again, I screamed. Nothing in particular. No words, just screaming. Maybe someone would hear me.

Suddenly it was as if heavenly Angels had stepped in on my behalf. Something happened, invisible to my natural eyes and yet visible in the men's actions.

I watched the drama unfold before my eyes. The men began to argue amongst themselves over my kettle. In the arguing I was forgotten. It was like they had been thrown into confusion and they could not agree on anything. They left me alone for a moment, as they were arguing about what to do next.

The leader summoned the others and told them, "Take what you can and get out of here!" Three of them went through the house, carrying out what they could.

They left the forth man, the rapist, who was now leaning over me, it seemed he was determined to finish what he had started. He stopped what he was doing and leaned out of the door. He listened. The others passed by him as they rushed out of the door.

The police sirens were coming nearer. Maybe he was assessing how close the police were. He listened. I listened.

It sounded as though they had found the correct street and now, they were driving down my road. I could hear the sirens getting closer. I was hoping they would not pass my house.

But they did. My heart sank. How long would it take them to figure out which house they needed to come to. As they continued to drive away, he leaned back inside.

Suddenly, he decided to give up. In a moment instead of

continuing with his actions, he looked down at me and gave me one last kick, but somehow, I knew his thoughts.

This is my first experience, after the near-death experience of reading someone's thoughts or sensing something that I could not have known. It was like I had 'super-powers'. Something deeper than a logical deduction. It was like knowing his thoughts. Telepathy. In the Bible it is the **"Revelation gifts" of the Holy Spirit.** The ability to read his mind. I anticipated the kick before he lifted his leg and so, as he lifted his leg to kick me, I kicked straight up, right between his legs, with as much force and strength as I could muster. It was a hard blow that made him buckle over. In a pained voice he swore at me and then he spat at me as he hobbled out the door clutching his groin.

I jumped up and ran outside for help. My friend shouted for me to come back and untie him, which I did. We both went out of the door.

I ran to a neighbour who said that he had not wanted to get involved. Had he heard my death screaming? Yes, he had. I was stunned. I replied, "couldn't you have at least called the police?"

My friend told me to go back inside, as he passed me. *(I had not yet realised what I was wearing)*.

The police arrived

The police sirens had headed back down the road towards us. My friend ran up the driveway and signalled for the police to come down to us.

There were two officers. A man and a lady. The lady officer who arrived was a familiar face for me. That brought a huge sense of relief to me, to see a familiar face – but also that she was a female. I'd just been surrounded by many men. It felt as if I was no longer outnumbered.

She suggested that she wait while I go and get dressed. I looked down and realised I wasn't wearing much. My T-shirt was ripped into pieces and covered in blood. I wasn't wearing anything else. My underwear had been cut off with a knife. I was naked from my middle to my feet.

She sat down on the bloodied couch, and I went into the bathroom. He gave his statement to the police. I didn't hear his statement. He was military trained. Very good at observation. Familiar with trauma. In control of his emotions throughout the ordeal. *He later expressed how his mind was trying to work out how he could get to the bathroom, to get the gardening spade that was waiting for me against the wall, so that he could have a weapon. In retrospect I'm grateful they didn't use it against us.*

I returned to the officer on the couch to give my statement to the Police.

She asked how long they had been there. I did not know what the time was. I told her that they had been there since around 5PM. She informed me that it was now almost 11PM. I realised that the ordeal had lasted about six hours in total in earthly time. I had not realised that the sky had turned black. Life had been a bit of a blur.

While the police questioned me, they asked how many men there were, and I said four. The police officer corrected me and told me what my friend had said, *"he says there were five. There was one that was standing watch over you the whole time."* I do know that there was one person watching over me, but he was not there *the whole time*. He was one of the four. I think he was the youngest, being given the easy job.

It occurred to me later that my friend had insect spray

sprayed into his eyes, right at the beginning of the ordeal. I did not receive any. His vision was probably blurry for most of the ordeal. He would have known if there were four or five. His observation skills were very finely tuned. I do not doubt that he had seen five 'beings.'

My eyes were not blindfolded from the beginning to the end, only for a short time during the ordeal. I had seen four *human* beings. I think that he saw *"the invisible one"* who untied the wire coat hangers behind my back. The hands that I had felt, but no one visibly standing there. I think this is who he saw *"standing watch over me the whole time."* I think it *was my guardian Angel* that I had not realized in the moment, was there. I had felt alone. I had been feeling like the only person who could help me was tied up under the table. That no one was hearing my screaming. That no-one was coming to save me.

After the Police questioning was over, I walked outside.

A young man arrived. I can't recall if it was Jason or Justin. I'll call him Justin. He came over to the house from a few houses away down the road and asked me, "Do you know me?" I said, "No." He said, *"Then why were you calling my name?"* I looked at him confused. I said, "I wasn't saying your name. I was just screaming." He looked puzzled and said, "You said *Justin Help me*, and I called the police."

Years later, I now have an explanation.

An Angel carried my screaming to his ears and said, *"Justin Help Me"* to him - after I asked God to *Please help me*. That was what the man heard, and he helped me.

I have often wondered who this young man was. God knew. He lived a few houses away. A young man, some kind person who called the police and helped save my life. The immediate neighbours could have called the police, hours before, but they told me that they had not wanted to get involved. When the police had driven up the road, they had driven past my house because they went to his house.

Afterwards my friend took me to the hospital in his car, which the thieves had been unsuccessful to steal, although they had attempted to.

In the hospital I required stitches. My mind downplayed it all. I thought maybe it happened when I was dragged across the floor by my hair. The answer came the next day when I returned to the cottage. The knife was lying there with my blood on it. I realised instantly with a shudder that I had been stabbed multiple times. I recalled lying on my back, like a tortoise stuck on its shell, with someone banging on my leg. At the time of being stabbed I was unaware of the blade or the pain. My focus was purely on survival, with resistance. Determination to keep them from raping me. When the young man said they would rape me, my resolve was to not allow it. I had fortitude. Resilience in my spirit.

The first night after the attack I slept at my friend's house. I knew he would understand that I did not feel safe at the cottage. I did not get much sleep. Every time I closed my eyes, I would see the gun in my face. It was a recurring shock wave. He was familiar with the process and explained what was happening to me.

In the end they never got away with much of my stuff, but they did take my guitar; which was a gift from my Dad; my clothes and all my underwear.

It was mild. I was fine.

At that stage they were hearing far worse crime stories; more shocking things happening to people in South Africa; things that you would not dream of knowing about.

> *"My grace is sufficient for you, for my power is made perfect in weakness" 2 Cor 12:9*

> *"God is our refuge and strength, a very present help in trouble." Psalm 46:1*

It will be a struggle

God used my Parents to lovingly help me to overcome the trauma that I had faced during the attack. I moved back in with them, back into the bedroom that I'd once shared with my sister. I was too scared to move into the separate garden cottage on the same property. I feared my own shadow and I was very jumpy. I was bruised and too scared to travel alone anywhere. My mother patiently accompanied me everywhere.

The paranoia lasted for weeks, months and eventually years. I went for counselling at my own expense. There is no such thing as the "government pays compensation" in

South Africa.

Initially, before the string of *"crazier than me"* counsellors, my Mom bought me a book to read. The author's story was about her being a victim of a violent crime that took place in South Africa. She was a young girl named *Alison*. In her story, she was "sexually assaulted" (that's the 'pretty' way of saying 'raped'). She was attacked by two *white* men. I think it was good for me to read that, if it was *blacks*, I may have developed a hatred for *all black men*. The two men slit her abdomen open after raping her and stabbed her multiple times. The stab to her throat allowed air down her windpipe so that she could breathe through the opening. Her story is called "I HAVE LIFE"[36] Alison helped me through my trauma. I was able to come out of my attack and realise that the one thing I had was MY LIFE. I had a second chance at life. I was alive. I decided the one thing that I was going to do for the rest of my life if I had breath, was Paint.

Journal South Africa 1999:

I'm going to PAINT WHILE I'M ALIVE! #paintwhileImalive

Why did the assault happen?

From my perspective it was a good thing. Not a pleasant experience but a worthwhile life (or after-life) lesson.

A loving father disciplines his children and brings them into correction by showing them RIGHT and WRONG.

I was on a path of self-destruction. Sin. Wilful sin and wilful disobedience.

I believe *absolutely* that God *allowed* the assault to happen. It was in place so that I could die, mercifully quickly, because God will kill the flesh to save the soul. I believe He instructed Satan to bring this on. There are examples in the Bible of Satan asking God if he can perform a certain task and God allows it within certain boundaries. God allowed it.

God has shown me tangibly His love and been like a faithful loving husband. I chose to continue into a path of wickedness and evil, *knowing it was wrong*. I was like an adulterous wife, unfaithful to Him, (with my nose piercing and being stabbed with blades) – read this passage. I see myself in it:

Ezekiel 16 allegory of Unfaithful Jerusalem paraphrased

"You were dying. I passed by and said LIVE!

When you were old enough for love I covered you with my love covenant and put a ring in your nose...

You made yourself a prostitute. You were unlike a prostitute because you scorned payment.

You degraded your beauty by offering your body with increasing promiscuity to anyone who passed by...

So, I stretched out my hand against you.

"I will sentence you to the punishment of women who commit adultery and who shed blood; I will bring upon you the blood vengeance of my wrath and jealous anger" 16v38

They will strip you of your clothes and take your jewellery. They will leave you naked and bare. They will stone you and hack you with blades...

I will put a stop to your prostitution.

Then my wrath against you will subside. My jealous anger will turn away from you. I will be calm and no longer angry.

22. INSIDE THE LIGHT

The white light He was surrounded by was a brilliant white but didn't hurt your eyes. I've come to calling this "the visible glory" or the "shekinah glory." — mentioned in Part 1 Seeing Jesus

So, I left my body I was instantly in the light. There was no tunnel or light at the end of the tunnel. I was completely in the light, and I knew that the light was Jesus…. He is surrounded by light. And when you look at the light, you see this ball of LIFE, but then you see this figure (man) coming out of the light. He is in the Light and He is the light.

JeffMara Podcast Transcript with clarification

I will explain some things about THE LIGHT, based on being in many discussions. Many more 'near-death' stories are surfacing, with modern medicine bringing 'dead' people back, as well as some preachers (genuinely, not the false ones), 'raising the dead.' I can attempt to tell you some things. I feel unqualified to speak about the Light. There is so much that I don't understand about the Light. The Light is so much greater than human understanding. English and I have limited vocabulary to explain spiritual things.

I know now, the Holy Qur'an speaks of God being Light, as does the Holy Tanakh and Holy Bible. I know now, that after NDE experiences NDE survivors come away generally, like myself, abandoning religious dogma, believing that religious practises are man-made folly. If you seek your reward from man in a religious organisation, you will get it there, but that is not an eternal reward. It will not do you any good once you pass away and enter your real reality. Earth reality is temporary. The Light, GOD, is above and beyond religious foolishness. His rewards are eternal.

God is in the Light. He is the Light.

It is my belief that we will all "see the Light." It doesn't matter who you are, you don't have to be a "Christian." I don't know how to explain that. I am talking about "seeing" the Light, not "knowing" the Light. If you want to replace the word here with "judgement": we will all face our own judgement. We will all be faced with seeing the Light.

Some people say they went to a "void" or had some other experiences. I am sure the researchers can give you far more information on the statistics. I'm an "experiencer" not a "NDE researcher." I think *the void* is different to what I am explaining.

I believe we will *all* get that opportunity, to see the Light. Not only "Christians" will see the Light. It's like facing God and facing our own reality. Facing who we really are. We are Light inside a physical temporary Body. It is like facing Life. We face the Life we have lived. (I'm not specifically referring to the 'life review' but there is that too). Seeing themselves as Light in the Light. It's a moment. That moment that you shift into that reality. All people have Light, are Light, and came from the Light. We don't all go back into the Light. Some people aren't ready to go back to the Light.

While on earth, not all people choose to walk in their Light nor in His Light while they are living this life, which is temporary.

The Light that we see is brilliant white, but it does not hurt your eyes. The Light appears to be made of a tangible energy. It is Energy. It is Life.

Some travelled down a tunnel towards The Light but did not enter the Light. Some told me that they believed if they entered the Light, they knew that they would not come back. God was very near to me at the point of death. I was *inside* The Light *and I came back*. Some did not feel One with the Light.

It is also my personal belief that we don't all **know the Light.** Saul saw the Light on the road to Damascus, but he did not *know* the Light. Relationships require spending time together and growing in relationship. When you face the Light, it's like Jesus says, "WHO DO YOU SAY I AM?" We will all face this question.

We will all face the Light whether we believe that **Jesus is the Light** is irrelevant to some extent. I've been told by others who have experienced NDE's (near-death experiences) that are non "Christian" nor "Religious" that "they have seen The Light" and they didn't know who the Light was.

Is Jesus going to say, "I never knew you"? Or does He know you?

I knew The Light. He knew me and I knew Him. I knew it was Jesus.[31] I know His voice.[15]

Before I got Baptised with the Holy Spirit, before 'I met the Holy Spirit', I did not know God. I knew *about* Jesus. I'd seen Him in a vision. I did not know The Word; I had not yet read the Bible. I did not feel my prayers were really being heard nor answered. I was saying them but to a distant far-off God. The Holy Spirit, 'the Spirit of Jesus,' some call Him, is in you when you invite Him into your life. When you accept Him. When you Believe. Therefore, they then say, "Jesus is *in my heart*." Jesus is in Heaven. But do you know the Holy Spirit? He is here.

I am the Light of the world – Jesus [31]

Every knee will bow, and every tongue will confess that Yeshua, Jesus, is Lord.[37]

23. THE UNIVERSAL LOVE

NDE's commonly experience a huge feeling of LOVE. To me the simple explanation is "God is love"[38] 1 John 4:8 It is the very essence of who He is, so of course, when they see 'The Light,' they will feel the essence of His love. He is a loving God! You commonly hear *"love and light"* – some people make out *that* is everything. It is only a *glimpse* of His nature! He is Love. He is Light.

In the Light people feel this "connectedness" - It is because of this "connected-ness" that I believe that we are called to LOVE ONE ANOTHER. We are connected to each other and what we do does affect the people and nature around us.

We are supposed to love ourselves, others and love God, the Master Creator. I think, so many people come back from NDEs and have a huge sense of love, but some turn it into a next type of 'religion' like a LOVE RELIGION (also known as "Tolerance" or 'not rocking the boat'). Others get so excited about being connected to the Light that they think they themselves are God, the source. *Nope I am not God, the Master Creator. I am a partaker in His nature, but I am not HIM!*

24. YOU ARE A MYSTIC!

"You're a 'new age' Christian!" "You're a Mystic!"

You cannot experience these things and *not* come out a mystic! Yet I am not a mystic either but sometimes it is easier to say that I am, instead of trying to explain. You cannot see things on "the other side" and come back unchanged. Your perspectives change because you have acquired new knowledge. The conservative church rejects most people who have experienced anything that does not line up with their dogma. But within Christianity, I found people who were embracing people like me, who had these newfound abilities of 'knowing' things or 'telepathy' after the NDE, and my other 'physic' abilities that I had from childhood. These things were accepted by these types of Christians. They are called, THE PROPHETIC, THE SEER, THE GIFTS OF THE HOLY SPIRIT.[39]

The Mystic awakening - Kabbalah

For me there was this forging of Christianity, Judaism, Jewish Mysticism (Kabbalah), but I still wrestled with religion. Religion is ugly. It causes wars. My experience in Jerusalem showed me that it was a very negative thing. I didn't want anything to do with religion. So, when people were saying to me, "your NDE is a *religious* NDE" and "you're just *religious*" I used to get so angry, and say, "I'm not religious." Funny thing is that the *religious Christians* I was being grouped with, reject me, and do not accept me because I am *"too rebellious",* and they see *"rebellion as witchcraft"* so they tend to group me in with the pagans. (Religious people did the same to Jesus).

I found a group of 'Modern' Christians who embrace "all things spiritual." They embrace and don't reject people who would be considered, "psychic, mediums, fortune tellers." They love them. They are not afraid of them, like the conservative Christians appear to be.

Now I am not saying that I agree with *everything* these 'modern' Christians say either! I'm merely saying that they exist. This group of people within Christianity who do not reject mystics. Some people call them "Christian Mystics" or "New Age Christians." There are "New Age" Christians, but to group all "spirit-filled" with "new age" is not the right balance.

I found a Christian book, not too long ago called "The Mystic Awakening" (Adrian Beale); he's basically teaching some Kabbalah (Jewish Mysticism) in that book.

Briefly Kabbalah is not *bad*. The Torah teaches us that we must not get involved in fortune telling and mediums and clairvoyants and all that kind of stuff. I agree. And so does Kabbalah.

In Kabbalah, the Torah and ZOHAR, are the main books that they use. Kabbalah is more about practical application than a head full of knowledge. Some things cannot be taught in books. They use the Bible, (the *Tanakh* and the *Torah*) and they have other books, like the Book of Abraham, (*Sepher Yetzirah*) which is the "Book of formation." Jesus did things that are normal in "mystical Judaism." He did things like walk on water and turn water into wine. He did things that were 'magical' and spiritual - but he did not do certain things that are forbidden in the Torah.

He taught us the mystical things that He did. **We can do what he did to some degree, under the Baptism of the Holy Spirit**. There were Messianic miracles that ONLY the

Messiah could do.

Kabbalah, Qabalah, Cabbalah

An overview of Kabbalah - **Kabbalah with a K** is Jewish mysticism. You've got **Qabalah with a Q** which sides with the Occult, witchcraft, and divination. They use the Kabbalah tree, and they add the pentagram into the Kabbalah tree, plus they have other practises. You have what they call **'Christian Cabbalah,'** which is Occultic - they don't necessarily speak Hebrew. Some things in these Christian mystic movements mix Kabbalah, Qabalah and Cabbalah together.

I don't know everything about it. I am still learning, and I started this journey in Tzaft (Safed), Israel in 1998.

25. THE ANGEL IN MY HOUSE

What about an angel showing up in the form of an angel?

I woke up at 3am. I looked across at the time and decided I would go to the toilet in the main part of the house, not the ensuite, so as not to disturb my husband.

I entered the toilet alone, and when I came out there was an Angel standing outside the toilet. I thought what lovely manners he had to not enter the toilet with me.

But then I thought, WHAT!

I wanted to defy what I am seeing so I decided to walk into it. He politely, gently stepped to his left. He remained there.

I stepped away and turned as I said "OK God, I am listening"

I went across to the dining room and took out my Bible and began reading. As I was reading a certain passage of scripture and the house was very suddenly struck with lightning. We hardly ever got lightning where we lived, so that itself, was unusual. The whole room lit up white with the light of the lightning. My eyes had been on this certain passage of Scripture, and I was still looking at it. Widow.

I understood that God was showing me something but sometimes we don't want to accept these things.

The next day I opened the Bible to further investigate the night before. My Bible was open on a passage that says God speaks through the thunder and lightning. [41]

That was enough for me to know that the experience was from God, even although the message was not pleasant for my human understanding.

I had wrestled with God, eventually I surrendered. The Lord had told me that I would be a widow. I said, "Your will be done My Lord."

Young single girls in church were always saying they were "waiting for their Boaz" - what a silly thing to say. In the Bible Ruth was married to Machlon and became a *widow* before she married Boaz. Who wants to be a widow? It really is not a pleasant thing to imagine.

26. OUR WEDDING AND HIS FUNERAL

The greatest gift God gave me was my husband, Riaan.

The husband "WHO'S NAME STARTS WITH AN R" was the man God had promised to send. We met, one month, almost to the day, after the home invasion.

He helped me to move back into my parents' home. The moment he crossed the threshold of the front door, carrying my baggage, my father knew. As I stepped in afterward, my father said, "THIS IS YOUR HUSBAND." I replied, "oh don't be silly I only met him yesterday!"

We were married.

I had slightly extravagant plans (not very extravagant) of where I had wanted to hold the ceremony, but my father-in-law suggested we hold it on my parents' property. All agreed, except me. (I had so much Pride). We held the wedding in my parents' garden on their property. They put in a huge amount of effort to prepare it for a wedding; repainted the old orange-brown house white and fixed up the gardens.

My dearest friend was living in New Zealand and could not make it over for the wedding. She sent a beautiful message which was read aloud to me by my new husband as a surprise; I (embarrassed to admit it) cried more over that, than his beautiful well-thought-out speech to me.

The photographer was the one thing we had invested a large amount of money on, (70% of our money available), believing it would be worth it because of his reputation and that after the wedding all you have left is the photographs.

He ended up irritating me throughout the ceremony, constantly telling me to go inside and fix my hair. (I think eventually my bridesmaid started to carry a comb with her) - and then he lost the photos! We received excuses and very few photographs. None of the bride and groom that I would enlarge and put into a frame. Even if I had wanted to enlarge a photograph, I could not do that. He retained the negatives that he had and offered no refunds. He gave us mostly a pile of photos taken of the entire group standing in a semi-circle in the garden. They were from a distance, so the faces are tiny. He was asking people to move around; he claimed later that at least we would know everyone who had come to the wedding. I guess he never realised how small the group was. We knew exactly who was there. Not a single photo of things like the bride with her mom, the bride with her Dad, the bride by herself, the bride with the Sister of the bride, her flower girl. About three close-up ones of the bride and groom *without other people* in the photo.

I gleaned as many photographs as I could from people who had taken a camera. My uncle passed away, but he may have had some good ones. I will never know.

I was very upset about the whole thing, for years afterwards. (Forgiven the photographer now, but it took many tears, as I sat scrapbooking my wedding album and coming to terms with the failed attempt of holding onto wedding day memories). It was not the "Cinderella fantasy" every little girl dreams of... And I was hungry. I had not eaten all day in the busyness, so by the end of it all I was tired and hungry.

As we were leaving, the photographer told me to lean across the "Just married" on our car... (written in black shoe polish) and well... that was printed across my white satin wedding dress! My husband drove around the corner and got the first wedding gift from me as his new bride – a hungry, tired, raving *lunatic* screaming and crying, wanting to rip my wedding dress into pieces.

My flower girl had gotten chickenpox, and on honeymoon I began to display that I had obviously contracted it. I was *very moody*.

A few months into the marriage I became pregnant with twins, and I was delightfully moody.

This poor man saw nothing but *the worst of me* from the day of our wedding – and yet he still loved me.

Two children later, God told me that He would be removing Riaan off the face of the earth in "ONE YEAR FROM NOW" (from then).

I begged for his life, and pleaded, *"God can you give him longer?"*

One year later I sat in the doctors waiting room, the doctor called me in. The nurse said that she would hold our third child, our baby daughter, for me while I went through. She insisted. I surrendered my little bundle and went in to see the doctor.

My husband was diagnosed with a brain tumour.

It was terminal.

I heard the words, "you need to prepare to be a widow…" and the rest was a blur.

PART 6: GIFTS FROM HEAVEN

Title: Download   Painted live for a fundraiser 2019

Love the Lord your God with all your heart and with all your soul and with all your mind and with all your strength" Mark 12:30

27. HEARTS FROM HEAVEN. EVERYDAY. OH, HOW HE LOVES ME.

Something that's happened since the home invasion, is that He, Jesus, He gives me a heart every single day!

It'll be like my kids will be spraying water and in their spraying the hose or something, I'll look at the ground and there's a heart or my daughter will come to me with chocolate and it's a heart or she'll make a little playdough heart.

It's like hearts from heaven. He has done it from 1999 until now is twenty-three years - every single day - Jesus gives me a heart. I don't ask for it. When it happens, I smile, "oh thank you" - He just reassures me that He loves me.

What about you?

What about YOU being the one whom He uses to bless others? What about being a gift giver. Giving away everything so that you bless someone else? Giving away your laptop? All your household goods? Have you given away a car or a house? Or start small, like giving away all your shoes except the pair you are wearing.

WENDY – BLESSINGS

Letting God supply

My God shall supply all your needs according to His riches in glory by Christ Jesus. Philippians 4:19 NKJV

Wendy's testimony

Some years ago, while involved in missions in central Africa, I had a significant blessing from Nathalie.

The previous year, my car had been stolen, on the day that I had just picked up 7 pairs of shoes that I'd had re-heeled and repaired.

I was living without any income, living by Faith. One evening Nathalie was hosting our Discipleship gathering. At the end of our time together she indicated that she had some things for me. She gave me 7 pairs of shoes that fitted perfectly, some body cream and writing paper - these 3 items were what I had asked God for that day.

I believe in Nathalie's kindness to give into my life, she was an instrument of God to meet the needs I had.

Nathalie — **OBEDIENCE IN GIVING** God told me to give away almost all my shoes to Wendy. I offered them to her and was surprised, we were both the same size. For me that was confirmation.

TRUST ME FOR PROVISIONS Toothpaste was one of those early things I learnt to trust God for, but what about other things and bigger things?

RICE. Another example of *almost spontaneous* provision. I was cooking and thinking, "rice would be nice" with the meal. A lady arrived at door with rice wondering if we would like some free rice.

A MICROWAVE. My Mom visiting us in New Zealand and saying she missed having her microwave, as I did not have one. I looked up to heaven and prayed, "Lord, you heard her" I said out aloud. Knowing that I could not do anything about this request, but He could. We were given a microwave within an hour! – knock-knock at the door – someone had emptied a storage container and wondered if we could do with a free microwave.

A FAMILY CAR. We had a normal 5-seater sedan, but there were six of us. My husband and I and four children. The backseat was only big enough for two. New Zealand were very strict about children being in car seats. The approved car seats were bulky, taking up the place of the seat and you couldn't squeeze another child into the seat, never mind another two children!

One day a lovely lady said, *"You've learnt how to trust him for aeroplane tickets, now you need to learn to trust him for a people mover"* – Sure enough she was right! I hadn't even thought of stretching my faith to believe for a car! We needed a van to seat, then six of us. As she called it, "a people mover."

My process was not very good. I was struggling to believe God for a car. I was not stretching my faith. I was looking at all the natural ways I could get money for a car. Eventually I repented. God has never once told me to get the money I need for something. He has always provided the "something" that I needed without any of my money.

I became aware one day while walking around the shops, that if you walk into a bicycle shop you don't say, "I want a bicycle" the shop owner will automatically say "and?" You are super specific. The shop assistant will expect that you have done your research and know what you want. Is it for a girl or boy. Is it for off road? Is it... you get the idea. A lot of thinking goes into it BEFORE you buy the bicycle. You walk in with some idea, and they help you narrow it down. Or you may even walk in knowing EXACTLY what you are looking for and see if they can accommodate or order it in for you.

I became aware of what I liked. I began to say, "I need at least a six-seater. I'd like silver or white. I'd like to be able to drive it." (I'm tiny... short girl problems, I would need to be able to see where I was going in it).

A lady and her husband called us and asked if they could drive by one Sunday after church and bring us something. They didn't say it was THEIR CAR. When they arrived, she apologised for her disobedience! Wow. She had felt to call me on the Thursday but was wrestling with God about handing over their car to me. *That Thursday had been my birthday!*

They gave it to us for free. FREE. They wouldn't receive any money for it. They said that they needed to obey the prompting of God.

It cost me $9 to put it into my name.

He has given me such incredible birthday gifts!

WHAT ABOUT MY 25th? It was a delightful surprise! I was invited to a "birthday banquet" dinner in California to celebrate a church's anniversary, they were celebrating it on the *exact day of my 25th birthday*. Dressed in an evening dress and heels I entered, and it was majestic: **"HAPPY 25th BIRTHDAY!"** signage was everywhere. Wow God! You knew I would be there at that *exact* moment, that year, on that *exact* day.

My 50th? *Adventures in the light* is launching in celebration of my 50th It is my gift to the world to open my heart and share this book with you and others, because I know my stories help people. I cannot believe it's been 25 years since I was in California hearing God telling me to write my book, *Discovering and Artist*. I wonder what God will do for my 50th. I'm nervously expectant, excitedly hopeful, knowing that **He will do something good** to surprise me!

He always does!! Wonders on wonders, it's sometimes hard to explain how wonderful He is!

2022. FOOD in abundance. The Butcher bird landed on my head, while I was talking to a lady about seeing her the next day. The next day when I arrived, she filled our van with food because more was coming to them the next day! She had a huge over supply and gave us a generous amount of food. God filled my pantry. God gives to the giver!

ALIDA – BLESSINGS

When the Butcher-bird visits

Alida's testimony

For many years, hubby and I were interested in listening and watching NDE accounts. The podcast of Jeff Reynolds (JeffMara podcast) became our favourite.

I was reading a book but true to human-fleshly nature, my ability to concentrate does wane, to my frustration, and I need to interpose my reading with something else sometimes. I had this one JeffMara NDE account pushing its place into my YouTube feed, just sitting there. I decided to listen to it. I felt a connection through the title: She had an NDE during a home invasion. 'Home invasion' being a terrifyingly familiar term for any South African.

Nathalie mentioned Brisbane in the podcast and my heart jumped with excitement that meant she may be living close to me! I sent a message to the email address she provided, including my phone number. I left it there, hoping – but not expecting - to hear from her.

The next day, the miracles began. Nathalie phoned me and the connection was immediate. While we talked, she mentioned that a bird just came to sit right on her head! It was a Butcher bird. We arranged to meet, and I believe both of us could feel that somehow, Divine Guidance is involved.

With our first visit at my house, a Butcher-bird kept flying in underneath our verandah and sat singing his lovely chatter like song so loudly that I had to really focus to listen.

Nathalie and I realised there is something to this. It is a message to pray! Since then, it has been proven true between us that this bird is a token for me to intercede, for it shows up every time when a situation occurs which needs intercession.

The Butcher-bird is a shrike, a species of birds having this harsh name given by humans, only because it stores it's catches of insects (and lizards) on spikes or branches or thorns to later feed to its chicks. (*It fills up its "pantry" for later.*) This is a very sweetly natured, but misunderstood bird. Nathalie has mentioned in her book "*Discovering an Artist*' the experience of being misunderstood. *(She purchased my book. I delivered a copy to her the first day that we met.)* Some circles reject the message she stands for, rejecting and misunderstanding her as person, together with the message of Divine Love.

Jesus is just SO AWESOME and life with Him, so much fun!

This morning, the Butcher-bird visited me again ... time to go pray ...Thank You, thank You Jesus for giving us life YOUR way.

Nathalie – **OBEDIENCE IN GIVING** I see Alida and her husbands' obedience to follow the Holy Spirit's leading and to be open to going above and beyond in service to

Him.

My story about Alida and I, 'from my perspective.' I went on the JeffMara podcast and had a flood of messages. It was a joy to reply to people.

Then one day the Podcast was removed by YouTube and now has a warning placed on it that it is 'restricted'. Jeff had warned me about the possibility of this happening, so during the interview I was very careful not to say words that may cause it to be censored. All went silent. For 24 hours I heard nothing. No messages and the video was down.

Then in my email popped a message from Alida. I went to check YouTube and discovered my video was back up. I replied to Alida that I would connect by phone the next day at lunch time. I immediately sent a text (S.M.S.) to her number from my number, so that she would be reassured if I didn't call, she had my number. The next day at lunch time I walked outside to call her and as I was talking to her a bird landed on my head. It then went across to our washing line. I thought "wow that was unusual" and told her immediately about the bird. We arranged to meet the next day. As we were leaving, she skimmed through her home and gave us some food from the overflow in her home. For her it was overflow, for me it was a confirmation from the Lord about a word He had given me about my new season.

The Lord knows that we have never had too much stuff but always, for 23 years, had "just enough" - we have never not had, but only had 'just enough' for the next meal, the next day, the next step, placing one foot in front of the other. He gave me a word that went like this, "YOU ARE USED TO HAVING JUST ENOUGH, BUT I WANT YOU TO GET USED TO HAVING MORE THAN ENOUGH." Since that word we have started to get food in our cupboards. We haven't rushed out and done panic buying, like everyone else through the pandemic, we have lived with 'just enough' but somehow by the end of the week there has been more than enough. When someone has stayed over for a meal, there has been 'more than enough' That day he filled my pantry. To me the Butcher bird was a symbol of God storing up food into our pantry, the way the Butcher bird stores up food for later.

28. HEALING IS FOR TODAY

Peter the Poet

> A MAN CAN FIX A POET'S SHOE
> BUT WHO CAN FIX THE POET,
>
> WHO?

I'll tell you as I told Peter the Poet in Israel:

"The answer is Jesus; The Healer can fix the Poet"

Nathalie - **A WORD OF KNOWLEDGE** I offered the advice or answer to the question. (THE WORD OF KNOWLEDGE from the Holy Spirit to increase his faith) because I KNEW the answer. He took it to heart as leading that was coming from God.

AARON SALISBURY – HEALED HANDS

Pastor healed by God of severe dermatitis

Transcript

"Gooday Nathalie, it's a real privilege to be able to just take a few moments to talk about what the Lord did when you gave me that word about oranges and vitamin C around my hands.

I can honestly testify and tell you that was an authentic and real miracle that God did there.

I have not had any dermatitis on my hands, at all since you gave that word.

I've been keeping up in my vitamin C and eating a lot of citrus and so on as I've been going along.

I just want to encourage you that that word was sound. It was good; and the manifestation is in my hands today. I am completely dermatitis free from continual dermatitis, continual problems. My hands used to bleed from the loss of skin on my hands. I hated shaking peoples' hands, or touching anyone else, because of the abrasion that came from my hands. I want to just encourage you with that, the Lord worked, the Lord used you. Be encouraged.

How long did you have that skin condition?

Well, that will be 20 years – it was a real miracle"

Nathalie – **A WORD OF WISDOM** God told me lay hands on Aaron's hands and to pray over his hands to receive healing. (THE GIFT OF HEALING). I offered the advice (THE WORD OF WISDOM from the Holy Spirit) to increase his Vitamin C because that impression came to my mind. He took it to heart as a word from God.

29. THE KEYS

KELLY – PROPHETIC ART

"I know when I met you, I was shaking all over."

Kelly's testimony

31 July 2014 a Facebook memory popped up reminding me of the first tree that I painted with you, that day in the Art class where we met each other. I recall that you said that my style of painting reminded you of Vincent van Gogh.

That art class was God's divine connection. I had wanted to paint. I had no foundation, no formal painting training. I had taken Art as an elective in high school, but we mostly drew.

A mutual Christian friend told me about you. God put us together. On the first day, at the first art lesson when I met you, I got the Holy Spirit shakes. I wasn't sure why.

I struggled through prophetic art. We did prophetic art together. It was a journey. We both got to paint. We had opportunities to do live painting together. We built our friendship. You get me, I get you.

God's goodness. God's ability to put people together that fit together.

You've been a strength. You are a strong person. Reliable. Generous, you give. You were someone I needed; the Lord knew that I needed. Encouragement. You have fully encouraged me above and beyond in art. You've never given up on me. You are just consistent. You pull out the gold. I love that about you. The Lord puts people in my life to pull the gold out of me we both needed that.

I want for you to take off, to flourish.

Nathalie – **PROPHETIC ART** – DISCIPLESHIP: To train up.

God gave me a handful of Art students. Kelly was the only student in that group, that I allowed into my personal life, to cross over that imaginary threshold of "client" to "friend." I saw in her someone who was not earthly minded but someone who had a heart after the things of God. I pulled her alongside as my apprentice and dragged her into art classrooms, halls, live painting sessions and eventually onto the stage with me. The day we met she had painted a tree. In all our time together, she painted one other significant tree. It was a dead tree standing in the cold winter snow. While it was only one painting, across years, it was a "prophetic art" painting that held many lessons, lots of patience and was release for her soul.

It is my belief that my story holds a KEY for some people. After painting keys, with my friend Kelly at an event, I suddenly felt prompted to "PUBLISH DISCOVERING AN ARTIST NOW;" then I felt "IT HOLDS THE KEYS TO UNLOCK PRISON DOORS AND SET THE CAPTIVES FREE." I had waited for nine years since I had first sat down and wrote the complete draft. For nine years I'd been editing it, editing my life. Forgiving. Healing. Moving forward. That book is the launch pad into this one.

For one, it will unlock something hidden inside you, like a young girl in Israel who had her Art unlocked; to another, it will open your eyes and give you a new perspective on something. For another, it holds a message of hope. For another, clarity. For another, Salvation. There are others that I wrote this book for, and I hope it reaches them and that they open it and read it. Whatever golden keys you found along the way as you read, I hope you picked them up. I hope you *use the keys* that you are being given.

THE KEYS TO THE KINGDOM

I summarised "The Prayer of repentance" [21] [22] into **A.B.C.D**:

ACCEPT, BELIEVE, CONFESS, DO

ACCEPT that Jesus is God [21]

BELIEVE in your heart that God raised Jesus (Himself, in the form of a man) from the dead. [21]

CONFESS with your mouth that "Jesus is Lord." [21]

DO whatever He tells you to do. [22]

"Surely God is my salvation; I will trust and not be afraid. The LORD, the LORD himself, is my strength and my defence; He has become my salvation." Isaiah 12:2

Isaiah 22:22 Key verse for this year 2022

They year of getting the keys.

THE KEYS TO GROWTH

G.R.O.W. It's like my A.B.C.D. – I adapted it slightly from the original.[42]

G – God first always put God first. Based on 'Seek ye first the kingdom of God' It's a verse we sang a hymn that stuck in my head based on Matthew 6:33

R – Read the Bible (start there)

O – Others (Go to church, wherever He leads you. Where you have peace. Let your inner Peace be your guide.)

W – Wear it or Witness (No I'm not saying become a "Jehovah's Witness," but to live a life that is a witness to others of your changed life. Alternatively, Ephesians chapter 6 speaks about "putting on the whole armour of God" – wearing it!

THE MOST IMPORTANT KEY: Receive the Holy Spirit

When the light comes, so does the heat!

– TD Jakes

Do your own research. When the Holy Spirit came it was recorded in the Book of Acts. You can turn to the book of Acts and just start reading the whole story. He never left.

He is a gift to us from Jesus. *"I will ask the Father and he will give you another Counsellor to be with you forever – the Spirit of Truth. The world cannot accept him..."* John 14:15-16

See also John 14:26, John 15:26, John 16:7-11, Romans 5:5, 1 Thessalonians 4:8 Luke 11:13 Acts 11:16-17 Acts 15:8

The Holy Spirit speaks Acts 13:2

Available now? Joel 2:28-29, 2 Peter 3:8, Hebrews 13:8, Acts 2:39

Jesus is the baptiser who Baptises us in the Holy Spirit. Matthew 3:11 Mark 1:7-8 Luke 3:16 John 1:33; Matthew 28:18-20

With the BAPTISM OF THE HOLY SPIRIT comes the GIFTS OF THE HOLY SPIRIT and Speaking in tongues.

THE GIFTS TO THE CHURCH

Romans 12:6- Gifts of the Father to the church

SERVING, TEACHING, ENCOURAGING, GENEROUS GIVER, LEADERSHIP, SHOWING MERCY.

Ephesians 4:11-13 Gifts of Jesus to the church

FIVE-FOLD MINISTRY: APOSTLES, PROPHETS, EVANGELISTS, PASTORS, TEACHERS.

1 Corinthians 12:4-11 Gifts of the Holy Spirit to the church

WORD OF WISDOM, WORD OF KNOWLEDGE, (special kind of) FAITH, HEALING, WORKING OF MIRACLES, PROPHECY, DISCERNING OF SPIRITS, SPEAKING IN TONGUES (in my opinion and experience, this is supernaturally 'other languages'), INTERPRETATION OF TONGUES (prayer language)

THE KEYS TO SUPERNATURAL PROVISION

Now faith is the substance of things hoped for, the evidence of things not seen. Hebrew 11:1[33]

The MAJOR KEY is FAITH.[33] Understanding that it is a "substance" in a sense, that you can grow. It is grown by *hearing and hearing the word of God.*[34] This is called "meditation on the word." Take God at His word. Believe His promises. You need to read the promises *and speak it* out, write it out and read it all over and over, until it drops from your head into your heart.[32] This is a spiritual principle that works, that is why people have "affirmations." They 'write the vision down' on a vision board, or in a place where they can see it, and then they *repeat it out aloud*. Their belief grows. *The mouth tells the mind what to believe. Watch out what you are saying!* My next book in process, is called FAITH LESSONS. I teach more practical lessons on how I grew my faith.

Without faith it is impossible to please Him Hebrews 11:6

Forsaking

All

I

Trust

Him

PART 7: CONCLUSION

30. APPOINTED TIME TO DIE

> *Each person is appointed to die once*
> *and after that face judgement.*
> Hebrews 9:27

NDE stands for NEAR-DEATH EXPERIENCE many people who "died" say that they "died" or "crossed over" or "went beyond the veil" - to name a few expressions.

I think that if you "enter the spiritual realm" or go through a type of "veil" separating the "natural" realm from the "spiritual" realm, I'd say that you go "beyond the veil"; that this can be done by people *without* a 'near-death experience'.

When I have an 'open vision' I feel like I have had the veil removed for that moment and I am *seeing 'beyond the veil'* into the other realm.

To me "crossing over" means that you have travelled "across the bridge into the Light" on the other side. Some people say they travel upwards, some say through a dark tunnel toward the Light. I say, across a bridge. Maybe it's a bridge, a tunnel or maybe it's a lake or body of water with a ferryman. It's "a something" between here and there. You *know* when you have stepped on the bridge, gone through that tunnel. You know.

Some people believe that if they had gone across that bridge into the Light that there was no coming back. Others like myself feel that we did cross over a bridge, into the Light – and then came back.

So, "Death" is something *beyond* that. Something beyond "Crossing over." Something that no one this side of death can *truly* know. Once a person goes beyond that point, they don't come back. Then they are dead. *Gone* from this realm. *Completely.* (Or not. It depends on a few things, like what you believe.)

The bullet did not go *through* my head, so some people feel that I was not *"dead enough"* to call it a "NDE." People comment silly things like this. Do they not understand that NO ONE who has truly "crossed over" *completely* is going to come back to give them a lesson on the "beyond"?

I didn't call my experience an NDE. I reported it to a

research group, and I was told about "near-death experiences;" led to the beginning stages of "finding my 'tribe'."

People are given information in the Light that they can come back with, like a second chance or a continuation. You get others, who use the term "walk-ins" as I am not a "walk-in." I do not feel qualified to talk too much on it, but do I believe it exists? Yes. In this sense, I was a Soul being given a chance to "walk-in" back into my body, to continue my "cycle." The concept of a "walk-in" is *"Gilgul /Gilgul nashamot/ Gilgulei Ha Nashamot"* ('cycle' 'souls').[40] It is the concept of the soul returning to continue; perhaps "walking into" a different body altogether. This is also known by some as "reincarnation", although that term is explained differently by different people. The Kabbalistic text which teaches the deep complex laws is not a text that I have studied. Some Rabbis reject the teaching of reincarnation altogether and others do not. The concept is not a punishment nor a virtue but rather a process of *"tikkun"* (rectification): *being given the opportunity to rectify.*

I came back into my body but within one year my entire

life was completely different. Then I was given a new name, a married name. My identity was completely changed in this realm. My purpose completely shifted from being single to that of becoming a wife and then a mother. Within a few short years, my citizenship was changed to a whole new continent and country. Physically your body changed too with childbirth. (And with age the hair turns grey!)

I felt like a soul in a cycle, in a process of rectifying something, completing a task. I was the same soul, but I went through a massive amount of change immediately following the assault.

31. THE GREATEST GIFT HE GAVE ME – MY HUSBAND AND CHILDREN

Jesus saved the best wine for last in the miracle at the wedding in Cana where He turned the water into wine. Wine that had not been pressed by humans on earth, but heavenly wine. Wine that was so good! I have decided to save the best testimony for last.

> *"I came so that you may have life and have it more abundantly"* – Jesus[32]

Husband's testimony

RIAAN COLIN DE WET

I'm the lucky guy who married this crazy woman. I'm joking! Let me let my husband speak for himself in his own words!

Riaan's testimony

It all started with a headache. A very average malady, experienced by millions of people every day and one that I decided to ignore and ascribe to everyday work-related stress. However, the average malady never cleared itself up and only increased in severity with each passing week. My laissez-faire approach to my health and wellbeing caused severe anxiety for my beautiful wife. She begged and pleaded with me to seek medical intervention but being a stubborn male, I was convinced that I knew better and that everything was going to work out just fine.

It took a telephone call from my mother, arranged by my caring wife, to compel me to agree to visit our local doctor. That was on the Sunday afternoon. I had planned to go to work as usual on the Monday and then visit the doctor during my lunchbreak. I never made it to my lunchbreak. My headache reached an excruciating crescendo on Monday morning. The pain was so severe and intense that I could hardly function. The best analogy I can think of to describe that awful moment is to imagine having your entire head squeezed by a malicious vice grip. Unrelenting pressure squeezing every vein, nerve, and fibre in your head. There is no release just continuous pressure and pain.

The Doctor examined me and sent me to Ascot Hospital for an immediate CT scan. The radiologist took one look at my scan and with an ashen face advised me that the images were not looking good.

I needed to complete a further MRI scan with contrast in order to have a full and clearer picture of what was troubling me. As I laid inside the bowels of the MRI scanner, motionless and silent, listening to the loud and repetitive clicking of the machine, I couldn't help but think that the confined space was somewhat similar to that of a coffin. Not a very comforting thought at the time and not the best way to celebrate my birthday.

The Radiologists verdict was grim. I had a very large tumour neatly nestled next to my brainstem. He looked at my wife and spoke directly to her. She had to expect me to experience seizures, severe mood swings and ultimately death. I read the Radiologists name badge, Dr. Hope. We were being informed of the worst possible outcome, but still here before me was the simple word HOPE! I am a visual person and seeing that word at that time was no coincidence.

That evening was a very low point in my life celebrating my birthday with a brain tumour. Here I was in New Zealand. A foreign country that I had just immigrated to. A relatively young man thirty-two years of age, married for six years, with three young children aged five, two and three months. I am a very practical man. I always hope for the best, but plan for the worst. My mind was swimming that night with thoughts and planning of things that I needed to put into place that would provide the best outcome for my young family if the worst happened to me. Questions of how, what, where and why needed to be answered. However, despite my fears I still had the glimmer of HOPE.

Time was of the essence. I had my emergency consultation with the neurosurgeon Mr. Bok the very next day. Once again GOD's mercy was evident. Mr. Bok was a fellow South African expatriate. Raised and educated in South Africa. Someone who I could relate to and someone who I could respect and trust.

I was diagnosed with a schwannoma. A rare type of tumour that forms in the nervous system. It was serious. I needed to have surgery as soon as possible since the tumour was pushing my brainstem to one side and it could be fatal. The tumour was in a very delicate part of my brainstem and even though it could be removed, it was anticipated that I would have permanent nerve damage. Damage, that could affect any number of my senses and bodily functions. There were just no guarantees of the outcome. I was scheduled to have my surgery in nine days time at Ascot Hospital and was sent home with a prescription of the steroid Dexamethasone to assist in reducing the swelling and inflammation caused by the tumour.

GOD was with me during those nine days before my surgery. Reminding me of HIS Word and helping me to reflect on things that I needed to correct in my life. I repented of my sins. I made right.

My wife was instrumental in arranging the Pastor and the elders of our local Baptist church to pray for me, to lay their hands on me and to anoint me with oil. I have no doubt that this action was a pivotal moment during this physical, mental, and emotional trial. GOD's will be done. I had peace.

I was admitted to Ascot Hospital and was pleasantly surprised to be informed that I had been appointed a private room that had previously accommodated Keith Richards, from the Rolling Stones, when he needed to recover from his head injury. Once again GOD's mercy was evident. The nurses that were appointed to my room were also expatriate South Africans. Ladies who could relate to me and make me feel comfortable.

I was prepared and wheeled into surgery. Mr Bok smiled at me as I drifted into sleep. The surgery lasted for eight hours. I awoke while lying on the bed with the hospital orderly pushing me out of the surgery and into the main corridor. My wife was the first person that I saw with my eyes as I exited the surgery. I could not speak, but I could show her a thumbs up hand signal as my bed was pushed down the hospital corridor toward the intensive care unit.

My time in the Intensive Care unit was a brief blur. All that stood out for me was enjoying seeing my mother, who flew all the way from South Africa, and my wife and my baby daughter beside my bed. Mr Bok confirmed that the surgery was a success. The tumour was also benign. He was able to remove the majority of isthe tumour with the residual remaining tissue unlikely to cause any further harm.

However, despite the good news I did incur nerve damage. My speech, balance, and ability to swallow had all been affected. My next two weeks in hospital saw me having to learn to swallow food and to walk again. Despite these impediments my spirit was not downcast but filled with a deep sense of gratitude and relief. GOD is indeed good. HE answers prayer and shows mercy.

I was immensely grateful to the hospital staff for their

care, but I was so eager to go back home and to be surrounded by my family and to sleep in my own bed. However, in order to achieve that I needed to be able to walk, use the rest room and swallow solid foods unaided. I was determined and resolute and with the grace of GOD I was released from hospital within two weeks from the date of my surgery.

I had completely lost my voice. My wife bought a red whistle for me to use whenever I needed her or someone's attention. However, despite this setback I was able to return to full-time work, much to the surprise of my surgeon Mr Bok and my Doctor. I was informed that generally an individual recovering from significant brain surgery takes months and even years to fully recover.

I was referred to a clinical voice and speech therapist. My throat and vocal cords were thoroughly examined. I was informed that one of my vocal cords was permanently lame because of nerve damage. It was unlikely to recover. I could undergo reconstructive surgery, but the outcome could not be guaranteed. I opted not to undergo the surgery.

I learned to live with my impediment. A year passed. Winter came and I contracted the flu. My throat was inflamed, swollen and soar. I coughed and I spluttered for a week. Then it happened. On my birthday sound returned. As my symptoms improved and I recovered from the flu. I started to speak in a very raspy, low hushed tone. Slowly at first, but then stronger and clearer with each passing day. There is absolutely no medical reason why my voice returned in the manner it had. GOD is the worker of miracles. HE showed me mercy and restored that which had been taken from me. My voice returned to normal.

Sixteen years have passed since that fateful day. I am grateful for everyday that I have been granted. I am a witness to GOD's infinite mercy and HIS healing power.

Nathalie – LAY HANDS ON THE SICK AND ANOINT THEM WITH OIL

> *"Is any one of you sick? He should call the elders of the church to pray over him **lay hands on him and anoint him with oil in the name of the Lord.** And the prayer offered in faith will make the sick person well; the Lord will raise him up" James 5:14-15* [33]

From the day we met Dr. Hope until the brain surgery was a total of ten days. I recognised ten as being the number of testing our hearts. Ten commandments. Ten plagues. The Tithe is a tenth of your income to give to God.

At the time we attended a local church. It was a Baptist church that did not believe in the "laying on of hands," nor the "anointing with oil." They believed that in the above verse was "the prayer of faith" would make the person well. I believe on the other hand that 'the anointing breaks the yoke of bondage' and the 'laying on of hands' imparts the healing miracle from the Lord. Forever grateful to our friends Wendy and Aaron Salisbury, who called me on the phone with this verse to "request the elders of the church come and pray" over my husband. When the elders came, they refused to use oil and I was so unbelievably angry. I fetched the olive oil from the kitchen and demanded that they 'do what is written'. They refused still. Then the young youth Pastor, Andrew, said he would do it. The others were angry with him, but he did it with me and the older men prayed. My husband felt the anointing for the first time. The heat of the Holy Spirit. He knew that God had touched him.

When the ten days were over, he went into surgery.

He came out alive and recovered, going from strength to strength.

I did not need to proceed with any funeral plans. The Lord had said to me, "I WILL GIVE HIM LONGER, AND I WILL GIVE YOU GRACE" Thank you Lord.

32. COMFORT IN DEATH

I've had many opportunities to bring people comfort through my testimony, like a mother whose son was murdered. She was tormented by a nightmare, feeling that he had been in so much pain as he was being stabbed. I could explain in detail how I felt when I was being stabbed.

Knowing so many people in South Africa have lost loved ones to unbelievable slaughtering, it's a burden on my heart to reach them. If you lost someone to a tragic death and you're upset and feeling that they felt the pain, I want to reassure you that they probably didn't! I hope my story gives you a little comfort about death, knowing that "the process of dying and the soul leaving your body" isn't "painful" in the way you think it is. The Soul slips out of the body instantly and is away from the physical pain. Whatever is going on with the body doesn't matter anymore. For those who have believed in Jesus, your soul is heading towards Him, The Light.

I am certain of this.

33. THE MEANING OF LIFE

When you get a second chance at life, you think about how you want to spend it. Old ideas die. Old dreams die.

You get a new reality about what the true meaning of life is.

This is what I learnt from my journey and experiences:

<u>The Meaning of life</u>:

We are here to learn to LOVE

Love God

learn to

Love Yourself

so that you can

Love Others

And as Dad said,

Be nice

<u>Our Personal purpose</u>:

Each Soul has been given a purpose.

This is based on your unique talents. What you do naturally that you just do, like water off a duck's back. Do what you were created to do.

Death is the only certainty in life,

We will all die.

The next time I go, I'm not planning on coming back.

REFERENCES USED/STUDY GUIDE

Scripture taken from THE HOLY BIBLE, NEW INTERNATIONAL VERSION ® Copyright © 1973,1978, 1984 by International Bible society. Used by permission of Zondervan Publishing House. All rights reserved.

Unless otherwise stated or paraphrased.

This is not my personal preferred Bible version; but it is with thanks to the above, that I may quote from this version for most of this content. I use a concordance and Bible dictionary alongside in my personal studies.

BOOK REVIEWS

Please email them to nathaliesstudio@gmail.com

TESTIMONIES

Wayne Dale – GIFT OF FAITH Dale Equine Dental Care cc, South Africa. "But without faith it is impossible to please Him." Hebrews 11:6 Word of ENCOURAGEMENT

Aaron Salisbury HEALING MIRACLE. Word of WISDOM Receive the Prophet and receive the Prophets reward. Aaron recognises the Prophetic gift in me and encourages it.

Peter the Poet – Israel Word of KNOWLEDGE

Maree Dobbs – New Zealand (Catholic testimony)

Heidi – Australia DELIVERANCE (Depression testimony)

Wendy Whalley Salisbury –Gifts from heaven

Alida Pretorius – used in Gifts from heaven

Kelly Whitehead – Australia (Prophetic Art testimony) used in Gifts from Heaven - The Keys

Riaan Colin De Wet – Husband's testimony used in Gifts from heaven

PART 1: FIRST BEING IN THE LIGHT

1. Seeing Jesus
   Extract taken from Discovering an Artist Chapter 8: THE ONLY WAY IS UP – Revised and expanded

   1. Definition "tutelary" – Dictionary/Wikipedia

   Because you have seen me you have believed. Blessed are those who have not seen me and have believed. John 20:29

   A WARNING FROM JESUS

   Matthew Chapter 24 Jesus speaking of the end times

   OPEN VISIONS

   2. When Steven was being stoned Acts 7:54-8:2 (7:56)

   3. The Introduction of THE FINAL QUEST by Rick Joyner. (page 9 and 10) Whitaker House 1996 ISBN 0-88368-478-0

   "I saw heaven" by Dr Roberts Liardon has a good explanation of "open visions."

   4. OBE definition Dictionary/Wikipedia OBE (Out of Body experience): "An out of body experience is an experience in which a person seems to perceive the world from a location outside of their physical body."

   5. Theophany definition Dictionary/Wikipedia

   SPIRIT-BODY/LIGHT-BODY

   Info on the Zulu Google African tribes and their beliefs

PART 2: JESUS

2. Would the real Jesus please stand up
   CHRISTIANS AND JEWS

   6. The Lord's Prayer Matthew 6:9-13

7. James 1:13-14

3. The Good Shepherd
    8. John 3:16

    9. Psalm 68:4

    10. Exodus 3:14

    11. John 14:10-11, 6,7

    12. HOLY TO YAHVEH Terrye Goldblum Seedman ISBN 1-883928-18-4 YAHSHUA and RUACH HA KODESH

    13. The angels are always saying, 'Holy Holy Holy' before the throne Revelation 4:8, Isaiah 6:3,

    14. 'Heaven was silent for half an hour.' Revelation 8:1

    Matthew 27:51-53 Quoted – dead that were raised

    15. John 10:1-18 NIV The Good Shepherd and the Sheep know his voice

4. The harmony of the Gospels
    16. ARIEL'S HARMONY OF THE GOSPELS Based on A harmony of the Gospels by AT Robinson by Dr Arnold G. Fruchtenbaum TH. M, PH D ISBN 9778-1-935174-62-2, and the Life of Messiah from a Jewish frame of reference.

    Quoted: Matthew 7:7 A.S.K. Ask Seek Knock.

PART 3: MY BACKGROUND

5. Imaginary friend
    17. Imaginary friends definition/ Wikipedia

    18. Atheism dictionary/Wikipedia

    19. Psalm 14:1 Fool says, "There is no God."

    "Art should comfort the disturbed and disturb the comfortable." – Cesar A Cruz, Mexican Poet often credited to Bansky in a meme (instead of Banksy – letters are the wrong way around – and it wasn't him who said it.)

6. Into the forest
   Psalm 42 quoted AMP version

7. My Church History
8. What is being born again?
9. Water Baptism
   Psalm 121:1 NIV quoted

   21. Romans 10:8-10 ACCEPT BELIEVE CONFESS

   22. John 2:5 DO WHATEVER HE TELLS YOU TO DO

   23. John1:12-13 It's not human decision that gets us 'saved'

   23. Hebrews 9:22

   24. John's Baptism different meaning to the Jewish, per Dr A.G. Fruchtenbaum

   25. Hebrews 12:2, 1 Corinthians 9:24-27, Hebrews 12:1-12

10. Baptism of the Holy Spirit
26. GOOD MORNING HOLY SPIRIT Benny Hinn ISBN 10 0 8 50092299 (1990)

27. I began reading little booklets that TJ introduced me to, by Kenneth Hagin Snr. Word of Faith movement.

   Holy Spirit John 14:15-16 See also John 14:26, John 15:26, John 16:7-11, Romans 5:5, 1 Thessalonians 4:8 Luke 11:13 Acts 11:16-17 Acts 15:8 The Holy Spirit speaks Acts 13:2 Available now? Joel 2:28-29, 2 Peter 3:8, Hebrews 13:8, Acts 2:39 Jesus is the baptiser who Baptises us in the Holy Spirit. Matthew 3:11 Mark 1:7-8 Luke 3:16 John 1:33; Matthew 28:18-20

   Receive the Holy Spirit

11. Catch the Fire
    28. The Foundations of Christian Doctrine by Kevin J Conner B.Th., M. Div., Th.D. (Hon). Bible Temple Publishing, Portland Oregon ISBN 0-914936-38-7 Printed in the USA (Kevin J Conner,

Melbourne Australia)

29. "Catch the Fire" then is not the same as "Catch the Fire" now. Catch the Fire' was a movement within the Toronto Airport Vineyard Church, it has been renamed "The Toronto Blessing"

12. The gold dust stories
30. "Golden Glory" - Ruth Ward Heflin ISBN 1-58158-001-0 McDougal Publishing page 23

13. Perspective
31. He is The Light. John 8:12; 1 John 1:6-7; John 9:5; Revelation 22:5; John 1:1-5; John 12:35-36; Matthew 5:14-16; Luke 2:32; Isaiah 9:2; Psalm 27:1; Isaiah 60:1-3; Isaiah 42:6; Psalm 23:1-6

PART 4: ANGELIC BEINGS IN THE LIGHT

14. Angels on the ceiling
15. Going to Hawaii
Extract taken from Chapter 10 United States of America - Discovering an Artist. Revised and expanded on explaining the supernatural side of the experience. Some parts excluded.

Quoted: "A double minded man is unstable in all his ways" James 1:8

Quoted: My God shall supply all your needs according to His riches in glory by Christ Jesus Philippians 4:19 NKJV

32. Walk by faith and not by sight 2 Cor 5:7

Conversion rate of the United States Dollar to the South African Rand was between 4-5 times. This means it was nearly 5 times harder for me to earn enough money. USD300 = ZAR1500 approximately.

33. Faith: believing what I couldn't yet see. Heb 11:1; 2 Cor 5:7

34. Faith comes by hearing and hearing by the word Romans 10:17

Quoted: Hebrews 11:6

YOU HUSBAND IS NOT HERE: Prophet David MacDonald. David McDonald Ministries.

16. A leap of faith
    Quoted: Hebrews 11:6

17. The centre of the world
    Israel 1998. Trip is mentioned with more details in Discovering an Artist.

18. Would the real God please stand up
    35. New American Standard Bible®, Copyright © 1960, 1971, 1977, 1995, 2020 by The Lockman Foundation. All rights reserved. 1 Kings 18.

19. Religion is messy
20. The dark side
    Jesus cast out demons

    Quoted: don't shout at devil Jude v 9-10

    Quoted: Ezekiel 16 Unfaithful Jerusalem.

PART 5: THE LIGHT

21. The near-death experience
    *Charm is deceptive, and beauty is fleeting; but a woman who fears the LORD is to be praised. ³¹ Honour her for all that her hands have done, and **let her works bring her praise at the city gate.*** Proverbs 31:30-31 (NIV)

    36. I HAVE LIFE Alison's Journey ISBN 014 028079-0

    Extract taken from Chapter 13: Unlucky 13? - Discovering an Artist. Revised and expanded on explaining the supernatural side of the experience

22. Inside the Light
    Jesus is the Light John 8:12b

31. He is The Light. John 8:12; 1 John 1:6-7; John 9:5; Revelation 22:5; John 1:1-5; John 12:35-36; Matthew 5:14-16; Luke 2:32; Isaiah 9:2; Psalm 27:1; Isaiah 60:1-3; Isaiah 42:6; Psalm 23:1-6

15. John 10:1-18 NIV The Good Shepherd and the Sheep know his voice

37. *Every knee will bow, and every tongue will confess that Yeshua, Jesus, is Lord. Romans 14:11*

23. The Universal Love
    38. Quoted: "God is love" 1 John 4:8

24. You are a mystic!
    39. Spirit-filled churches -Bethel Church and the like – NAR churches (New Apostolic Reformation), Revivalist churches, Word of Faith churches. The churches that get a bad name in media!

    40. Kabbalah text - Book of Abraham, (Sepher Yetzirah) which is the "Book of formation"

    40. ZOHAR - Kabbalah text

    40. "Gilgul /Gilgul nashamot/ Gilgulei Ha Nashamot" (cycle souls) – Kabbalah Mystic terminology for the reincarnation or incarnation of souls. The Kabbalistic text which teaches the deep complex laws of Gilgulim, Sha'ar Ha'Gilgulim, (Rabbi Isaac Luria and Rabbi Chaim Vital)

    40. Tzaft (Safed), Israel

25. The angel in my house
    41. Job 37

26. Our wedding and his funeral

PART 6: GIFTS FROM HEAVEN

Love the Lord your God with all your heart and with all your soul and with all your mind and with all your strength" Mark 12:30

27. Hearts from heaven, everyday Oh how he loves me

My God shall supply all your needs according to His riches in glory by Christ Jesus. Philippians 4:19 ᴺᴷᴶⱽ

Wendy testimony

Alida testimony

28. Healing is for today
29. The Keys
    Kelly's testimony

    Isaiah 22:22 Jesus holds the KEYS. 2022

    Keys to the Kingdom ABCD

    21 ref and 22 ref

    "Surely God is my salvation; I will trust and not be afraid. The LORD, the LORD himself, is my strength and my defence; He has become my salvation." Isaiah 12:2

    Keys to GROW

    42. G.R.O.W. - I'd like to credit David Salisbury. It's my understanding he taught this to pupils and through one of them, I came to hear of this. (He said it came from "The four spiritual laws") David and his wife, Lynette were a missionary couple in Zambia, Africa, with their children.

    Keys RECEIVE THE HOLY SPIRIT

    John 14:15-16; See also John 14:26, John 15:26, John 16:7-11, Romans 5:5, 1 Thessalonians 4:8 Luke 11:13 Acts 11:16-17 Acts 15:8; The Holy Spirit speaks Acts 13:2; Available now? Joel 2:28-29, 2 Peter 3:8, Hebrews 13:8, Acts 2:39; Jesus is the baptiser who Baptises us in the Holy Spirit. Matthew 3:11 Mark 1:7-8 Luke 3:16 John 1:33; Matthew 28:18-20

    GIFTS TO THE CHURCH

    Romans 12:6- Gifts of the Father to the church

    Ephesians 4:11-13 Gifts of Jesus to the church

1 Corinthians 12:4-11 Gifts of the Holy Spirit to the church

KEYS TO SUPERNATURAL FAITH

33. Hebrews 11:1; ref 34; ref 32

Without faith it is impossible to please Him Hebrews 11:6

PART 7: CONCLUSION

30. Appointed time to die
    Quoted: *'Each person is appointed to die once and after that face judgement.'* Hebrews 9:27

31. The greatest gift to me – my husband and children
    Testimony of my husband, Riaan Colin De Wet - 5 August 2022

    "I came so that you may have life and have it more abundantly"

32. Comfort in death
33. The Meaning of Life

May your find the source of my strength on these pages

My other book, Discovering an Artist,

Paperback   ISBN 978-0-6487484-0-3

eBook   ISBN 978-0-6487484-1-0

Also available through my linktr.ee/nathaliesstudio

CONTACT THE AUTHOR

For speaking appointments, please contact the author directly.

Nathalie de Wet Diploma Secretarial, Diploma Art & Creativity (Hons), Certified Interior Designer and holds other certificates.

Queensland, Australia

through email: nathaliesstudio@gmail.com

You can connect with Nathalie through Linktr.cc/nathaliesstudio

her Public Facebook page:
www.facebook.com/artistnathaliedewet/

through Instagram: www.instagram.com/nathaliesstudio/

ABOUT THE AUTHOR

Nathalie de Wet was born and raised in South Africa. She is a survivor of a life-threatening attack. She understands the power of overcoming hatred; racial, towards the opposite sex and self-hatred. She understands what it means to live under strong controlling fears, panic attacks and through post-trauma stress (PTSD).

She also relates to women who've been told that they would not be able to have their own children. Her message is: there is hope and healing available.

Nathalie has had supernatural encounters with a God-Man-being, she calls Jesus and believes Him to be the Jesus, spoken of in The Holy Bible, the one in 'the forbidden chapter' Isaiah 53 Tanakh, and the Isa ibn Maryam of the Holy Qur'an. This Jesus is not a respecter of persons. She believes that He is divine, healed in Bible times, is risen and alive, still healing people today. He has healed her.

Nathalie has sold her artwork across the world since 1996. She has won art awards and International art awards, including a first-place National art award in New Zealand (2005). She loves to paint.

She currently lives in Australia with her husband and their five biological children.

www.ingramcontent.com/pod-product-compliance
Lightning Source LLC
Chambersburg PA
CBHW041429300426
44114CB00002B/9